It would be a total travesty if this book was dedicated to anyone but the man who faced every sink full of washing up, every sticky surface and a constantly exhausted wife with equanimity and calm. To Bob.

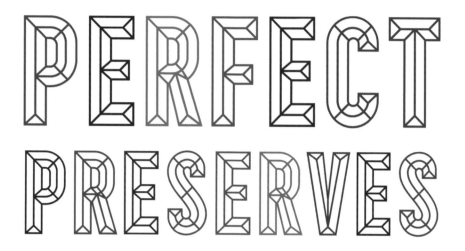

PERFECT PRESERVES

Thane Prince

HODDER &
STOUGHTON

Contents

Introduction

I am often asked when it was I first began my love affair with preserving and, thinking about it for a while, I realise that I have been fascinated by jars of jams, jellies and chutneys since I was very small. The craft of preserving and stocking the pantry was an integral part of my childhood, when my mother would follow the seasons, pickling, bottling and potting whatever could be safely stored away to enliven our food in the bleak North Norfolk winters.

I loved to help and not only because I was a hungry little girl; it was more than that. I'm sure my affection was based on the love and security that comes with a shared task, the filled shelves and the glow of an important job well done, as much as a promise of something sweet for my tea.

Little did I realise then how important preserves would become to me, not only to feed my family or as gifts for friends, but also in my role as Preserves Judge on *The Big Allotment Challenge*. It was whilst working on the show that the idea of this book came about. Spending time with passionate gardeners and seeing just how prolific the crops they grew were, I couldn't help but envisage the jars of spicy chutneys, tangy pickles and smooth-as-silk curds that could be made from all this wonderful bounty.

Talking to people about the show, I noticed that many found the idea of making even the simplest of jams daunting: they worried about such complexities as pectin in fruit, what vinegar to use for pickles, how to make even a simple jar of lemon curd. *Perfect Preserves* is my answer to those questions. Here is a book that takes you by the hand and leads you through the door into the wonderful world of preserving.

At the start of each chapter you will find a master recipe, one that tells you everything you need to know about how to make a perfect jar of jam, chutney, curd or pickle. Each recipe is thoroughly explained, including exactly what equipment you might need, the steps you need to take, and what problems to look out for. Let me say here that there is very little equipment that you won't already have in your kitchen, and so you can get started straightaway.

My idea is that even the novice can make a perfect jar of each type of preserve in the book by following the step-by-step instructions. Once you are confident with the techniques, you can graduate to the recipes that follow the master recipe. Using the same methods you will soon become adept at preserving, and before long you will be adapting the recipes to suit your and your family's tastes, using whatever fruit and vegetables you grow in your garden, pick from your allotment or buy at the local market.

To start the book there is a glossary of all the things you need to know, in which technical words are clarified, and ingredients explained. Here you can find which fruits contain high levels of pectin, which sugars to use in jams, what acidity vinegar needs to be for pickling, and much, much more.

I have had a wonderful time writing this book, as it has reinforced my love of preserving. I've come up with some delicious new recipes, and tweaked some old ones to make them even tastier. I am now besotted with gooseberry and elderflower curd, and have a range of fruit ketchups sitting alongside bottles of cordials that will take the flavour of summer on into winter.

I began writing this book when Seville oranges were in the shops. Each year I wonder at how simply splendid it is that, in January's darkest days, these glorious oranges fill our kitchens with the smell, taste and colour of Spanish sunshine. From citrus fruit to the first, palest pink champagne rhubarb, and here a tribute to our Victorian forefathers who, using ingenuity, new farming practice and a keen eye on profit, formed the Rhubarb Triangle in Yorkshire, where this premium fruit is still grown. Soon after these we have elderflowers and heady perfumed strawberries, crisp radishes and bright green beans. Before you know it, we'll be in autumn, with all the wonders that season provides.

Throughout the year, using the fruit or vegetables that are most abundant in that season, I make one or two jars of my favourite preserves. These will not only help keep the joy of the seasons alive, but also feed that hungry little girl who still lurks within.

Glossary

ACID When making jams and jellies, one part of the equation is the acidity of the fruit. This has to be right to bond with the sugar and pectin to ensure a set. A simple guide is: does the fruit taste roughly as sour and acidic as lemon juice? Gooseberries, raspberries, currants and cooking apples when boiled all taste very acid, as do most citrus, but other fruits will need additional acidity.

The easiest way is to do this is to add freshly squeezed lemon juice or use the equivalent amount of citric acid. 1 teaspoon citric acid powder when dissolved in 50ml water is the equivalent of 2 tablespoons of lemon juice.

Juice from high-acid fruit can also be used, with redcurrant or gooseberry juice being the most useful.

APPLES Packed full of pectin and acid, apples are a very useful fruit in preserving as they can be mixed with fruit lower in both these necessary components. You can use both cooking and eating apples in preserves. If you choose an apple that breaks down to a purée when cooked – a cooking apple such as Bramley, for instance – it can be added to sauces, jams and chutneys to add both bulk and texture.

Apples can also be cooked and the juice dripped through a jelly bag to use as a base for herb-flavoured jellies. Commercial apple juice can be used in some preserves.

APRICOTS These bright orange fruit are woefully low in pectin and acid, so will need both added when making jam. Fresh, they make a wonderful jam; dried, they contribute colour, sweetness and texture to both chutneys and conserves.

AUBERGINE I like to use aubergine in chutneys, especially those with a touch of Indian spice. Choose firm young aubergines: older softer ones contain more water which tends to lengthen the cooking time. I never salt aubergines before cooking.

BACON I use dry-cured, smoked or unsmoked bacon, made from the meat of rare-breed pigs. This is not fancy, it just tastes better.

BANANAS Use firm ripe bananas to make both jams and chutneys. Bananas are high in pectin, but low in acid.

BEETROOT Try to get medium beetroot, again choosing firm fresh specimens. If you are pickling beetroot, try to find small, evenly matched ones, so that they both cook at the same time, and look good in the jar.

BERGAMOT These fragrant citrus fruits are used to give Earl Grey tea its distinctive flavour. They make lovely jellies and marmalades as they are high in both acid and pectin.

BLACKBERRIES There is a difference between wild and cultivated blackberries. The latter are more luscious but have a milder flavour; wild blackberries have a lovely complex flavour, but are very pippy, so are best used in jellies.

BLUEBERRIES New to our shores, blueberries are now being grown widely in Britain. Blueberries are low in both pectin and acid, so both need to be added when making jam. Blueberry skins become tough unless the berries are cooked before any sugar is added to the recipe.

BOIL There are many different levels of boil used in preserving. You have a low simmer for cooking the fruit and vegetables, then a moderate boil for reducing chutneys, and a full rolling boil, one which cannot be stirred down with a wooden spoon, when cooking for a set with jams and jellies.

BOTTLES You will need bottles for cordials, liqueurs, ketchups and sauces. I buy new ones from an internet site (www.jamjarshop.com or www.lakeland.co.uk). You can of course re-use bottles provided they are well washed and sterilised in the oven. I have given volume measures in the recipes so you will need to assess how many bottles you need for each one. If you have no bottles you can use jars. All bottles for sauces and ketchups must have vinegar-proof lids.

BRINING The term used for soaking vegetables in brine, which is a strong salt solution. The prepared vegetables are soaked in it for a given number of hours. The usual proportions when making brine are 150g sea salt to 1.5 litres water.

Brine is easiest made using a small quantity of hot water to help dissolve the salt, then the remaining water in the recipe is added cold, to cool the brine. Brine should always be used cold to avoid encouraging bacterial growth.

Prepared vegetables should be placed in a clean glass, china or plastic bowl covered with the brine, and kept fully submerged by pressing them down under the liquid using a suitably sized plate.

After the given time, drain the vegetables, wash them well under cold running water then spread them out on a clean, ironed tea-towel or kitchen paper to dry.

BUTTERS Fruit butters are smooth spreads made from fruit and sugar, but containing no dairy products.

CARROTS Choose medium-sized sweet young carrots, which will be tender and delicious in chutneys and pickles. Carrots need very little brining.

CAULIFLOWER Firm medium-sized cauliflowers are best, and they should be used as soon as possible after they have been picked.

CELERY Firm young stems of fresh celery are best, and I like to de-string them using a potato peeler. This is not necessary if you are using the stems for a sauce or ketchup.

CELLOPHANE COVERS If you are re-using your jam jars, you may choose to cover the preserves with cellophane circles. These are widely available from kitchen shops and should be used with waxed discs for sweet preserves like jams, jellies and curds.

Immediately after you pot your jam or jelly, while it is still hot, put a waxed disc, wax-side down, on top of the hot preserve in the jar. You must make sure the whole disc touches the surface of the jam etc. and that there are no air bubbles. Take a small brush and lightly brush one side of the cellophane circle with water. Place this, wet side down, on the jar and secure with a rubber band, pulling the cellophane tight once the band is in place.

CHEESES These concentrated fruit jellies are made by cooking down a fruit purée until thick. They contain no dairy products.

CHERRIES Sweet cherries are low in acid and pectin, so both will need to be added to any jams you make with them. Morello cherries have a moderate amount of pectin and are high in acid. I use dried cherries to add texture and flavour to conserves and liqueurs.

CHESTNUTS In season from late autumn to January, sweet chestnuts make a wonderful vanilla- and brandy-laced conserve. I have given several ways to peel them with my recipe.

CHINESE LEAF This fleshy oriental leaf is most often used in kimchi, a Korean pickle. Buy fresh firm Chinese leaf from oriental supermarkets.

CHOOSING FRUIT & VEGETABLES FOR PRESERVES Always look for the best-quality fruit and vegetables you can find. Choose young, small perfect fruit for jams and pickles. Whilst you can use slightly less perfect fruit and vegetables for jellies, chutneys and fruit butters, it is pointless preserving anything that is second-rate.

Try to make your jams and pickles as soon as possible after your fruit and vegetables are harvested.

CHOPPING VEGETABLES You will notice I give exact instructions on how to chop vegetables in some of these recipes. The reason for this is threefold: an even chop will look better when you serve the pickle or relish; the vegetables will cook at roughly the same time; and the flavour is dramatically changed by the pieces being the same size.

CHUTNEYS These sweet-sour preserves use both fresh and dried fruits, vegetables and spices. They keep well and are eaten with cold meats and cheeses.

CITRIC ACID A useful addition to your store-cupboard, citric acid comes in powdered form. You can add the citric acid crystals as they are or dissolve them in water using 50ml per level teaspoon of crystals. 1 teaspoon in 50ml water is the equivalent of 2 tablespoons lemon juice.

CITRUS FRUIT Most citrus fruits are high in acid and pectin, the exception being sweet oranges. When cooking citrus for use in marmalade, you must make sure the peel is tender enough to cut with a wooden spoon before adding sugar.

CLEMENTINE A small, sweet, thin-skinned citrus fruit I use for marmalade. Clementines are usually coated in a thin layer of wax, so will need careful scrubbing with hot water before use.

CLOTHS Jelly bags, muslin, and tea-towels used in preserving should be spotlessly clean and scalded before use. To wash them, use a mild detergent with a little bleach added. Rinse well, then immerse in a saucepan of clean water, bring to the boil, and simmer for 2 minutes. Then drain the items and allow to drip-dry. Jelly bags, tea-towels and muslin can be further sterilised by pressing with a hot iron when dry.

COFFEE Choose freshly roasted beans, and grind them just before use.

COLLOIDAL BOND This is the proper name for the set that you achieve when acid, pectin and sugar are cooked together in the correct quantities when making jams and jellies.

CONSERVES Here I use the term to signify a softer-set, lower-sugar fruit preserve. Once open, conserves should be kept in the fridge.

CORDIALS These non-alcoholic concentrates can be made from a wide variety of seasonal fruits and flowers. They do not keep well so must be stored in the fridge or a cold outhouse. Dilute them to taste with fizzy or still water, adding ice cubes and some fresh herbs or lemon slices. In winter I use boiling water to make hot drinks.

CORNFLOUR Made from ground maize, cornflour is used to thicken relishes and some pickles. Mix the stated amount with cold water to give a runny paste then add to the hot relish, simmering for 3–4 minutes until no taste of raw flour remains.

COURGETTE Never think of making a huge batch of courgette chutney or pickle unless you are sure you can use it! Gluts are hard to deal with, but if you didn't eat the courgettes fresh, you're unlikely to eat them pickled. Choose small, hard courgettes that are bright in colour and freshly picked.

CRAB APPLES High in both acid and pectin, crab apples make wonderful pale pink jellies with only the addition of sugar. Usually collected as windfalls, be sure to discard any that are mouldy.

CRANBERRIES Available in late November cranberries add colour and texture to jams and chutneys. High in acid, but containing only a moderate amount of pectin, cranberries need cooking before the addition of sugar to make sure the skins are tender.

CUCUMBER There are two common types of cucumber: the long salad cucumber and the smaller ridge cucumber. Cucumbers are high in water, so will need salting to remove some of this. Ridge cucumbers can be bitter so always taste a small piece before preserving.

CURDS Curds are elegant sweet preserves, containing butter and eggs, which are best made in small quantities and stored in the fridge.

CURRANTS Small seedless grapes are dried to give currants. These are quite acidic and give a sharp ping of flavour to chutneys.

DAMSONS These are small, usually sour, plums useful for jelly making and flavouring liqueurs. They are high in acid and pectin, and only need sugar added.

DRIED FRUIT Sultanas, currants, raisins, prunes, apricots, figs are all used to add sweetness, texture and interest to a wide range of chutneys and sauces.

DRY SALTING Here prepared vegetables are sprinkled with fine sea salt that then leaches the liquid from them. In a large glass, china or plastic bowl layer up the prepared vegetables, and sprinkle each layer with a couple of tablespoons of fine sea salt. Cover the bowl with a plate and leave overnight unless told otherwise. Wash the vegetables well under cold running water then spread them on a clean, ironed tea-towel or sheets of kitchen paper to dry.

ELDERBERRIES Collect elderberries in late autumn and use for jams and jellies. They will need both pectin and acid added.

ELDERFLOWERS Pick elderflowers early in the morning on a dry day in early summer, and use to flavour cordials and jellies. I also use elderflowers in curds.

ENGLISH MUSTARD POWDER This bright yellow powder packs quite a punch so should be used with caution. Add it to piccalilli and other mustard pickles.

EQUIPMENT Most of the equipment you need to make the recipes in this book will already be in your kitchen: wooden and metal spoons, scales, knives, chopping boards, large pans etc. I don't use a sugar thermometer, so don't feel you need to buy one of these. A jam funnel is a useful and inexpensive bit of kit that helps keep the rims of your jars clean when you fill them. And if you're going to try your hand at making jellies, a jelly bag and stand are well worth investing in.

FIGS Fresh figs are wonderfully sweet but contain little acid or pectin, so both will need adding for fig jam. I use dried figs in relishes and chutneys, but as they are often coated in cornflour they will need careful washing before use.

FOOD PROCESSOR I have a wonderful food processor with several bowls and a purée attachment which makes many of the processes in this book simplicity itself.

FRUIT Choose good-quality fresh fruit for jams and jellies.
* High pectin fruit: Cooking apples, crab apples, lemons, Seville oranges, damsons, red plums, black- and redcurrants, gooseberries and quinces

* Medium pectin fruit: Bananas, raspberries, greengages, loganberries, sour cherries, cranberries, some sweet oranges
* Low pectin fruit: Wild blackberries, blueberries, peaches, pears, rhubarb, strawberries, sweet cherries, figs, melons, apricots

FULL ROLLING BOIL To give the freshest tasting jams, you need to boil the mixture as hard as possible for the shortest possible time, so you are looking for what is called a full rolling boil. This is when your pan of jam or jelly is boiling so hard the bubbles cannot be stirred down using a wooden spoon. It is because the mixture bubbles up when at a full boil that a large preserving pan is essential when making jams and jellies.

GARLIC Usually used fresh, garlic adds wonderful flavours to savoury preserves.

GINGER Ginger is used in both sweet and savoury preserves. It comes in many forms: fresh, dried, powdered, crystallised and preserved in syrup. I find the best way to peel fresh ginger is to scrape the skin from the tuber using the edge of a teaspoon.

GOCHUGARA This Korean chilli powder is used when making kimchi, a Korean pickle. Any chilli flakes can be used as a substitute.

GOOSEBERRIES One of the earliest summer berries, gooseberries are high in both acid and pectin, so they make wonderful jams and jellies. You must top and tail gooseberries when making

jam and cook the berries until the skins are soft before adding the sugar.

GRAPEFRUIT Thick-skinned, acid- and pectin-rich grapefruit make delicious marmalade. Usually covered with a fine wax coating, you need to scrub them well with hot water to remove this before use.

GREENGAGES This pretty green/ yellow member of the plum family is low in pectin and acid, so both will need adding for jam. You can make delicious ketchup with greengages.

HERBS Common herbs like rosemary, basil, mint, tarragon, bay, sage, thyme and oregano can all be used in preserves. Pick fresh herbs early on a dry day. They can be spread on paper towels and dried in a cool oven for later use.

JAM A fully set preserve, usually made with equal quantities of fruit and sugar.

JAM FUNNEL A wide-mouthed funnel that is used to fill jars and bottles.

JARS I use a wide variety of jars, some new and some recycled from previous preserves. These come, inevitably, in a variety of sizes, so I have chosen not to tell you how many jars to use in individual recipes. Jams and jellies are perhaps best in 200g jars, chutneys in bigger jars, and butters and curds make good presents when potted into small jars.

Make sure you wash your jars thoroughly in hot soapy water and rinse them well. Dry thoroughly and before use then sterilise them by placing them on a baking tray and then into an oven preheated to 100°C/200°F/Gas 2 for 20 minutes.

I also re-use lids, making sure they are in good condition. Because of their vinegar content, chutneys and pickles need vinegar-proof seals. Any lids with no rust or flaws, and with a thin plastic or rubber ring inside, will serve. If you use hinged glass-lidded jars, make sure you have a supply of new rubber rings available. Or you could cover your jars with wax discs and cellophane covers (see page 9), although this is not suitable for vinegar.

JELLY A clear preserve, usually made from fruit juice, that has a softish set: it will sit well on a spoon but shivers when wobbled.

JELLY BAG AND STAND If you intend to make many jellies it's worth investing in a jelly bag stand and a couple of bags. For occasional jelly making, you can improvise by dripping the juice through a fine woven cloth, such as butter muslin or an old tea-towel, hung between the upended legs of a stool.

JUICER If I'm using a small quantity of juice, say one lemon, I use a hand-held wooden reamer, sieving the juice to remove any pips. If, however, you need a large quantity, a juicing attachment for a free-standing mixer or food processor is very helpful.

KETCHUPS These fruit-based sauces tend to be sweeter and are eaten fresher than more traditional matured brown sauces.

LEMONS I use a lot of lemons in preserve making, as they are highly acid and their peel contains high levels of pectin. Please note there is little or no pectin in lemon juice. Lemons come in many varieties, with the best and most fragrant being the large, light yellow coloured ones from the Amalfi coast.

LIMES Choose the largest limes you can find. Pick those with a dark green skin that are firm to the touch. Kaffir limes, while very fragrant, are not very useful in preserving as they contain very little juice.

LIQUEURS Sweet, alcohol-based, fruit-flavoured drinks, liqueurs are typically served after a meal.

LIQUID SMOKE This is a commercially prepared condiment that adds smokiness to sauces and relishes.

MANGOES Look for firm ripe mangoes, and choose the largest ones you can find to give a better ratio of flesh to stone.

MAPLE SYRUP The concentrated sap of the maple tree, this natural syrup has a wonderfully complex flavor that can be used in both sweet and savoury preserves.

MARMALADES Preserves made from citrus fruit, where the peel is an integral part of the end-product.

MELONS Melons are very high in water and contain almost no acid or pectin. Choose fully ripe, fragrant melons, and use the sugaring technique (see page 19) when making preserves with them.

MIRIN An essential condiment in Japanese cooking, the rice wine mirin has a low-alcohol, high-sugar content.

MOULD Moulds are micro-organisms that are very difficult to kill. Which is why I urge you not to use mouldy fruit or vegetables for your preserves. On some fruits, especially apples, moulds can produce toxins which are not killed by heat. I would therefore suggest that, while I feel happy to spoon small amounts of mould off the top of jams, I would be very wary about moulds in any other circumstance.

OLIVE OIL Much has been written about olive oil, and it is often said that you should avoid cooking with extra virgin oil. I do not agree with this, so in this book I use a good-quality extra virgin olive oil, but not a single-estate one.

ONION An essential ingredient for most savoury preserves, onions come in many sizes and strengths.

ORANGE Oranges are generally high in acid and pectin and can make lovely preserves. There is no pectin in orange juice, it is entirely in the skin. Seville oranges are the famous bitter oranges commonly used in marmalade making and appear in our shops in January. Blood oranges are sweet oranges with red flesh that give a ruby-coloured juice. They are high in acid and pectin.

PASSIONFRUIT These exotic fruits are wonderfully fragrant. They contain very little substance so are usually combined with other fruit for preserve making. Passionfruit are delicious made into curd.

PEACHES Although low in both acid and pectin, peaches are delicious pickled in vinegar, steeped in brandy and made into chutneys.

PEARS To my mind these rather insipid fruits need quite a lot of seasoning to give something worth eating. I use them to add bulk to chutneys and jams. They are low in acid and pectin.

PEPPER, BELL Bell peppers add both taste and colour to preserves. I usually prefer to use fully ripe red peppers as I find them fuller in flavour, but both yellow peppers and green, unripe, peppers can be used.

PEPPER, CHILLI Green (unripe) & red (ripe) chillies contain varying amounts of capsaicin, the element that gives them their heat. Most of the heat is contained in the pith and seeds, so you can control the heat by the amount of these two elements you leave in or out.

PERSIAN ROSE PETALS Dried rose petals add elegance to jams and jellies. They have only a modest perfume and are usually used in conjunction with rosewater.

PERSIMMON The high tannin content of this fruit makes it totally unpalatable when under-ripe, but once ripened the fruit is amazingly sweet and tender. I use Hachiya persimmons for cooking, which are larger, more oval and pointed than the Fuyu fruit, which develops a deep orange colour with almost jellied flesh when ready to eat. Persimmons have many names including Sharon fruit and kaki.

PICKLES Whole or sliced fruit and vegetables preserved in flavoured vinegar.

PISTACHIO NUTS These lovely nuggets of green nut meat are often used in conjunction with dried fruits to make conserves.

PLUMS Most plums, when slightly under-ripe, are high in both acid and pectin, and so are excellent for jam making. Small plums are best made into jellies and savoury fruit sauces.

PECTIN When combined with sugar and acid, pectin – which is a naturally occurring soluble fibre – forms a bond that causes jam and jellies to set. The amount of pectin in fruit varies, so it is important to know whether the fruit you want to use has sufficient pectin to form a set.

If a fruit is low in pectin you will need to add it, which is easily done. You can use one of the three types of commercially available pectin: liquid, powdered and one where it is already combined with sugar (jam sugar).

If you prefer you can add pectin-rich fruits to those lower in pectin. For instance you can add an equal quantity of fresh grated apple to fresh strawberries.

Or you can make your own pectin. Blitz the shells of 2–3 unwaxed lemons with 500ml water, then simmer in a non-reactive pan for 10 minutes. Strain carefully – or drip through a jelly bag as you might a jelly – and add this pectin-rich liquid to your jam.

It is important not to worry about adding pectin any more than it is to worry about adding lemon juice or sugar – think of it as just another ingredient of the preserve.

POMEGRANATE This fruit gives a wonderfully rich red juice, which is acidic but contains no pectin.

POMEGRANATE MOLASSES This is the much reduced and sweetened juice of pomegranates, useful to add a sweet-sour flavour to preserves.

PRESERVING PAN When making preserves it helps to have a large heavy-bottomed pan with an acid-proof lining. This can be a dedicated preserving pan that can be bought from any good kitchen shop or online at www.lakeland.co.uk or you can use, as I do, my biggest cast-iron casserole dish with its enamelled interior.

Other choices can be a wide, deep, stainless-steel pan. It is helpful to have a lid that fits, but a baking tray can be called into action if your pan has no lid.

The pan needs to be deep enough for you to be able to boil jams and jellies at full throttle without them boiling over. It should also be as wide as possible, giving a large surface area that allows your chutneys, butters and cheeses to reduce more quickly.

Aluminium pans are not suitable for most preserves as the metal is not acid-proof. Hard anodised aluminium pans are fine.

Maslin stainless-steel preserving pans are widely available. They come in many grades of steel: choose the heaviest you can afford.

PRESSURE COOKER I find a pressure cooker useful when cooking more resilient fruit and vegetables like quince, beetroot and marmalade oranges.

PUMPKIN Choose dense-fleshed, deep yellow pumpkins to make fruit butters. I like to use Crown Prince or Butternut.

QUINCE A large, hard fruit that contains plenty of pectin but is low in acid. I find it best to cook quinces in a pressure cooker before continuing with most recipes.

RADISH Mouli or oriental radish and small red radishes add texture and crunch to mixed vegetable pickles and kimchi, a pickle from Korea.

RASPBERRIES My favourite summer fruit, raspberries come in many varieties. They have a moderate amount of both acid and pectin, so you can make a good jam with just the addition of sugar.

RELISHES These lightly cooked, crunchy, sweet-sharp preserves are best stored in the fridge.

RHUBARB High in acid but low in both pectin and sugar, rhubarb adds a lovely tang to both cordials and fruit butters. Early or champagne rhubarb, available in spring, comes from the Rhubarb Triangle in Yorkshire. It has a beautiful pink colour and high acidity. Garden rhubarb is best eaten early in the summer when it is still young.

RUNNER BEANS An allotment staple, pick beans for preserving when they are about 20cm long and before the beans inside the pods have begun to form.

SALT Salt is essential to preserving. It was one of the earliest preserving mediums, and was so highly valued in society that many words and customs surround its ownership and use: 'salary', 'below the salt', 'salting it away' . . .

Salt acts on food in two ways during preserving. The first is that, when used dry or as a brine, it leaches water from food, so drying it. The second is that it repels bacteria.

Salt comes in many forms, but all come from just two sources: rock salt, which is mined, and sea salt, which is collected by evaporation. I prefer the flavour of sea salt, finding it more delicate.

Coarse and fine salt crystals can be used in brining and dry-salting. Large salt flakes have a clean fine flavour, but are to my mind too expensive to use in preserving. Some flavoured salts are useful in preserving, smoked salt being my favourite.

Some table salt contains an anti-caking agent, usually calcium or magnesium carbonate. Whilst not harmful, I prefer to avoid salts with additives.

SALTING (see Dry Salting, Brining)

SAUCES Smooth and tangy, these bottled, vinegar-based sauces are best left to mature for several weeks before eating.

SCALES Correct quantities are important when making jams and jellies as the ratio of sugar to fruit reflects the final results. I use electric scales that can weigh both solids and liquids.

SCUM A rather horrid word for the whitish substance that forms on the top of jams and jellies as they boil. It is caused by impurities in the sugar and can be skimmed off once the setting point has been reached. Use a slotted spoon, rinsing between skims in a handy little bowl of hot water.

A tiny pat of butter can be stirred into the jam to get rid of any final scum.

If the scum bothers you, preserving sugar, a large-crystal, pure sugar, gives off very little scum, but is more costly than granulated. Raw sugars will give most scum.

If you add flowers, chopped herbs, vanilla seeds etc. to jams and jellies, do so after skimming.

SEEDS I buy whole spices whenever possible, and always keep the following seeds in my store-cupboard: celery, fennel, coriander, cumin, cardamom, mustard.

SHALLOTS Shallots come in many sizes and have a good rich onion flavour. Small shallots can be pickled in vinegar and larger ones used in chutneys.

SLOES Pick sloes late in the autumn from the hedgerow blackthorn bushes. They can be used for sloe gin, jellies and to mix with other wild berries to make jams and conserves.

SOY SAUCE Choose a naturally brewed Japanese soy that is not artificially coloured, as these sauces – and there are several available – have a more complex flavour. If you want your sauce to be wheat-free, look for Tamari soy.

SPICES I prefer always to buy whole spices where possible, then I can use them whole, crush them lightly or grind them to a fine powder if the recipe requires. Once ground, spices lose their flavours quickly, so if buying your spices ground buy in small quantities.

Amongst those I keep in my cupboard are smoked paprika, star anise, juniper berries, cardamom, vanilla, cinnamon, cloves, nutmeg, coriander, peppercorns, allspice berries, blades of mace, turmeric, cayenne.

SPICE MILL I use an electric coffee grinder that I keep solely for grinding spices, and so I avoid contaminating my breakfast coffee. You can buy spice mills that have two or more bowls, which are very useful.

SPOONS You will need a variety of spoons: a large, metal slotted spoon for skimming jams and jellies; some wooden spoons for stirring and for using the flake test (see Testing for a Set) for a set (I try to keep at least one spoon for fruit and one for onions etc. to avoid the flavours mixing); metal spoons of varying sizes for tasting; a set of measuring spoons for spices, salt etc.

STRAWBERRIES Possibly the fruit that causes most tears when jam making, strawberries are low in acid, sugar and pectin. Use just ripe, small berries from a fragrant variety.

SUGAR The use of sugar in home-made jams is necessary not only for achieving a set but also because sugar is a natural preservative that binds water to prevent the growth of micro-organisms, thereby helping to prevent spoilage in your jams and preserves. Using the right amount and variety of sugar is one of the most important parts of jam and jelly making. Which sugar you use influences not only the flavour of the finished jam but also the price per pot.

Whatever sugar you choose it must be fully dissolved in your preserve before the mixture comes to the boil to avoid any chance that the jam or jelly will crystallise. Timings involved in dissolving sugar will vary, according to sugar type, heat of liquid etc. You must check that the pan no longer feels gritty, and that there are no signs of sugar crystals on your wooden spoon before continuing with the recipe.

✳ White sugar: I have tried all types of sugar when making preserves and I find that granulated sugar gives as good a result as more expensive preserving sugars and it should be used in all recipes unless stated otherwise. Caster sugar has fine crystals and so is best used for curds as it dissolves quickly.

✳ Jam sugar: This sugar has already been mixed with powdered pectin in an agreed ratio. I have used jam sugar here for any recipe that needs added pectin.

✳ Preserving sugar :This is a white sugar with large crystals that dissolve slowly. It is said that using this sugar will mean that your jams and jellies have less scum, and that they will keep better. I have never found the extra expense worthwhile, but the choice is yours.

✳ Raw sugar: Light and dark muscovado, molasses and golden granulated can be used, but will make the preserves darker in colour and, if used to make jams and jellies, can mask the fresh flavour of the fruit. The exception is in a dark, full-flavoured marmalade: here I would usually opt for raw, unrefined cane sugar as it gives a more robust taste to the preserve. These raw sugars are also excellent when used in chutneys and pickles.

SUGARING This technique is used when the fruit is likely to break down a lot during jam making, or when you don't wish to add water to an already delicate flavour. Sugar toughens up cubes of melon and bananas, and the skins of strawberries, for instance, giving a better texture to the finished preserve. To sugar fruit it is first prepared and then layered with the sugar from the recipe in a large, non-reactive bowl. The bowl is covered and then put in a warm place for several hours, or in a cool place overnight. The action of osmosis pulls liquid from the fruit and the sugar begins to dissolve. Usually there will still be plenty of undissolved sugar in the bowl and so the fruit, juice and sugar must be gently heated in a preserving pan to fully dissolve the sugar before you continue with the recipe.

SULTANAS Sultanas add both texture and sweetness to chutneys and sauces. I usually chop them roughly before I cook them.

SWEETCORN Corn is best used as soon after it is picked as possible, for the sugars in the corn begin turning to starch once the cobs are separated from the plant, which changes the taste. It is important not to salt the water when you're cooking corn, as this will toughen the kernels.

TESTING FOR A SET I don't favour using a sugar thermometer so I use one or other of these two methods of testing for a set. Both are effective but for the beginner I think the wrinkle test easier to understand.

Before you start testing for a set you need to study your jam: it will begin to thicken a little round the sides of the pan as it reaches setting point. I have given approximate boiling times in these recipes but as all pans differ in size, and fruit in water content, the actual time your preserves take to reach a set may vary. Always turn off the heat while you test the jam.

✳ The flake test: Take a wooden spoon and scoop up a small amount of jam or jelly. Allow it to cool for a moment then gently tilt the spoon to pour the jam back into the pot. If the final part of the jam falls in a flake rather than a stream the jam is ready.

✳ The wrinkle test: Keep a supply of small plates or saucers in the freezer. Take a cold plate out and then spoon on about 1 teaspoon of hot jam or jelly. Allow it to cool – about a minute – and then push it from the side with your finger. If the jam wrinkles, it is ready. If not, put back on the heat before testing again.

THAI FISH SAUCE A fermented fish sauce, which is useful in oriental pickles. Fish sauce adds umami.

TOMATOES Tomatoes of all shapes, sizes and stages of ripeness are used in preserving. You must choose a suitable tomato: ripe red ones for ketchup, and large green ones for a green tomato chutney. Bear in mind that small tomatoes will have a larger pip and peel ratio to flesh.

To skin, cut a small cross in the base of each tomato and drop it into a bowl of boiling water. Leave for about 1 minute, and you will see the peel begin to come away from the flesh. Lift the tomato from the water using a slotted spoon, strip the peel off and discard it.

TOMATO PURÉE A concentrated essence of tomato, useful for adding extra flavour to a sauce.

TURNIP A useful vegetable to add crunch and texture to mixed pickles. Choose small turnips, picking them before they become woody.

UMAMI This is the 'fifth' taste which forms the palette of flavours that include salt, sweet, sour and bitter. Umami is found in ingredients that have aged, such as anchovies, soy sauce, Worcestershire sauce and Thai fish sauce.

VINEGAR Vinegar is a mixture of acetic acid and water and is created by the action of the bacteria *Acetobacter aceti* on ethanol, which is another word for alcohol.

Look carefully at the acidity of the vinegar when making brined pickles, as you must use vinegar of at least 6% acidity.

* Red and white wine vinegars are usually 6% acidity and are suitable for all pickle and chutney making. They have a good, clean flavour. I like to use white wine vinegar for most of my pickling.
* Cider vinegar has an acidity of about 5%. It has a soft, smooth taste and is an excellent choice for chutneys and similar preserves, but is not acid enough for pickles.
* Malt vinegars come from the brewing industry and can be either malted or distilled. They usually have an acidity of 6%, making them suitable for all forms of chutney and pickle making. Malt vinegar has a distinct flavour, while distilled vinegar is flavourless.
* Rice wine vinegar is a soft-tasting vinegar from the Far East. Like cider vinegar, it tends to have an acidity of only 5%, so pickles made with it will not have a long shelf-life and should therefore be stored in the fridge.
* Sherry vinegar and balsamic vinegar are good for adding flavour to preserves but I don't find them useful in pickling or when making chutneys.

WAXED CIRCLES These are used with cellophane circles to seal the lids of sweet preserves. The disc is placed, wax-side down (this is the shiny side) on the surface of the hot preserve. You must make sure there are no air bubbles beneath the wax. Cover the jars with cellophane as described earlier. There is no need to use wax circles when you are using lids with rubber or plastic coatings.

WORCESTERSHIRE SAUCE A British classic, Worcestershire sauce is a fermented condiment that adds umami, salt and seasoning to preserves.

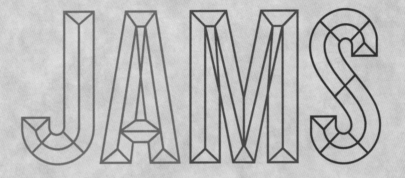

Perfect Jams

Jam is to my thinking the most lovely of all preserves. The simplest, purest jams are ones in which the flavour and perfume of the fruit is captured, literally preserved, to eat another day. A spoonful of raspberry jam on a winter's afternoon brings back the glow of summer gardens, a lava flow of rich, golden apricot jam atop a steamed sponge pudding adds sunshine to the darkest December meal, and a puddle of blackcurrant jam in a bowl of steaming porridge puts a smile on anyone's face.

Jam is not a necessary food but a luxury one, and this seems especially true when you look at the history of both jam eating and jam making. Think for a moment of how recent the universal availability of white sugar, or even sugar of any hue, is. Whilst sugar cane had been grown for many centuries in Asia, and was known in the British Isles since the time of the Crusades, it always had to be imported. As a result, its cost was prohibitive, so only the very rich could afford it. Growing fruits, especially exotic ones, was also the domain of the wealthy and the serving, cooking in sugar and thence the preserving of such rare and beautiful ingredients was therefore a true symbol of wealth.

These days we can all enjoy jam and this chapter has recipes for many of my favourites. There are rules when it comes to jam making as there are whenever sugar is used in cooking, but once you understand these rules you can experiment with flavours and spices, creating your favourite preserves to serve in triumph at your own table.

A FEW THINGS TO KNOW ABOUT MAKING JAMS

★ A jam is a set fruit preserve. By set I mean a preserve that mounds on a spoon, one that sits comfortably on a scone and does not drip from your breakfast toast. A set is achieved when fruit plus acid, sugar and pectin in the right proportions are cooked to a temperature and concentration that allows the formation of a colloidal bond. So essentially when the fruit is boiled with these three ingredients in the correct quantities, the jam will set. The question is, though, how do we go about getting the right mix? This is not as daunting as it sounds: many fruit are high in pectin and also high in acid, so sugar is the only part of the equation that needs to be added.

★ My first rule is that only perfect fruit should be used for jam. You are preserving an illusive flavour, and will work hard to make sure the jam is balanced and correctly set. Why then would you want the final taste to be of slightly mouldy berries? Avoid at all cost fruit labelled 'For Jam', as this is often over-ripe and beginning to soften or rot. For a chutney, jelly or even fruit cheese, you can cut away the bad parts and continue, but for jam you must use the best-quality fruit you can find.

★ Berries with a rich colour and perfume, but very slightly under-ripe, are best. Firm fragrant plums, apricots that still only just give when gently squeezed, and figs that have not split at the base are all excellent.

★ The pectin content of fruit varies enormously, with apples, lemons and gooseberries being high, and strawberries, rhubarb and apricots being quite low. For more information, check the individual fruits in the Glossary on page 8, which tells you which fruits are high in pectin and therefore which jams will need additional pectin.

★ For the acid part of the equation you must think about how sharp the fruit is. Is it as sharp as lemon juice, for example? No need then to add more acid. But if the fruit is palatable and sweet to taste, then you will need to increase the acidity to achieve that all-important set. Lemon juice is most commonly used for this purpose but on occasions I've used balsamic vinegar in a strawberry jam (see page 42), and you can use citric acid in its powdered form.

★ For a set jam the quantity of sugar is dictated by the quantity of fruit on an equal basis. Low-sugar jams are looser in texture and must be stored in the fridge (see Conserves, page 104). There are several sugars available to the jam maker. I favour white granulated sugar for the simple reason that it is the least expensive. I've used it in all my recipes for many years and have yet to find an issue with it.

★ If extra pectin if required for a jam then it's simplest use 'jam sugar' which has pectin ready added. You can of course add the pectin separately, and I do choose this route occasionally, but a ready-mixed sugar/pectin combination is the equivalent of baking with self-raising flour, which makes life much easier.

★ It is really important that you weigh your ingredients carefully. As a general rule I use equal quantities of prepared fruit and sugar, adding acid and pectin as necessary.

★ You will need a large heavy-bottomed pan. This does not have to be a dedicated preserving pan but it must be a pan that is non-reactive or acid-resistant. I use a giant enamelled iron casserole dish, but stainless steel is good also. Choose a pan that is wider than it is tall. A good surface area is necessary to allow for rapid evaporation of water when boiling for a set.

★ It is perfectly fine to re-use old jam jars and lids for jams, but the jars must be spotlessly clean and not chipped or damaged. Any lids must be spotless too, with no sign of damage or rust. And you can, of course, use waxed circles and cellophane to cover your jellies.

★ There are three basic methods of making your jam. By far the most common is to simply place the ingredients in your wide pan, put this over a low heat and stir the mixture until the sugar has completely dissolved. This is important, for if the sugar is not fully dissolved before you boil the jam the result may be a somewhat crunchy, grainy jam. Still edible but not a prizewinner.

★ A second method of making jam comes into play when the fruit you are using – cherries, cranberries, bluskinseberries, currants, to name but a few – have resistant. In these cases you need to cook the fruit in added water before the sugar is incorporated to ensure the skins are softened.

★ The third method of making jam is to 'sugar' the fruit. Sugaring is used when you are making a jam from wet, rather fragile fruit. I 'sugar' strawberries and melons. The process is simple: prepare the fruit and place it in a non-reactive bowl, then add the sugar. You can layer it, but I just give everything a good mix then leave the bowl in a warm place: the bottom oven of an Aga, a warm kitchen or an oven that is cooling after use, for a couple of hours. The juice will be drawn from the fruit and the recipe can proceed. This process helps fruit that are liable to collapse to hold their shape better: the sugar hardens the skins of, say, strawberries, so that you will have visible fruit in your jam. The juice from the fruit also begins to dissolve the sugar, giving a shorter cooking time to these fragile fruit. Sugaring can also be done overnight in a cool room.

★ Before boiling the fruit with the sugar, you must check that the sugar has fully dissolved. Timings for this vary, according to sugar type, heat of liquid etc. Check that the pan no longer feels gritty, and that there are no signs of sugar crystals on your spoon. If you can see crystals of sugar on the sides of the pan, use a dampened pastry brush to wash them back into the jam.

Have a bowl of cold water handy.

★ As with all preserves, you need to sterilise your jars and their lids. Do so by putting them on a baking tray and into an oven preheated to 100°C/200°F/Gas 2, and heating them through gently for 15–20 minutes. You want your jars to be hot when you are ready to pot your jam.
★ Once you are sure the sugar has fully dissolved, turn up the heat under the pan and bring the fruit mixture to the boil. Cook the jam

at a full rolling boil (see Glossary, page 13), one
that can't be stirred down with the spoon, for
5 minutes, stirring quite often to stop the fruit
catching on the bottom of the pan. I use a small
timer to remind me of how long my jam has been
boiling.

★ To make your first test for a set, take a plate
or saucer from the freezer and drop a spoonful
of jam on to it. Leave for about 1 minute then
push the side of the mixture gently with the
tip of your finger and look at the surface. If it
wrinkles, the jam is ready to pot. If the jam is still
runny, turn the heat back on and boil the jam for
a further 2 minutes before testing again. Always
turn off the heat while testing for a set. Repeat
the boil/testing process until the jam tests
positive for a set.

★ Once the jam has reached setting point,
turn off the heat. Skim off any scum that has
collected on the top of the jam, using a slotted
spoon, cleaning it in a bowl of hot water
between skims.

★ Leave the jam to cool for 5 minutes. Take
the baking tray of jars from the oven at the
same time, as they too need to rest for about 5
minutes.

★ When the jars are cold, label them, and check
the lids are firmly screwed on. Store in a cool,
dark place or, if you have one, a pantry or larder.

★ Pot the jam into the hot jars. I use a jam
funnel to help with this, but a ladle is fine. Top
with the lids.

How to Make the Perfect Jar of Plum Jam

Plum jam is the simplest jam to make. Plums are high in both pectin and acid, and are readily available in late summer and into autumn. A note here: not all members of the plum family are the same, so greengages and apricots will need special treatment when making jam.

Yield approx. 1.2kg | *Keeps* 9–12 months

Ingredients
1kg red plums
250ml water
900g white granulated sugar

Equipment
Measuring jug and scales ★ Some glass jars with lids, washed and dried ★ Baking tray ★ 2–3 small china or glass plates or saucers ★ Colander ★ 1 clean tea-towel Chopping board and sharp knife ★ Large heavy-bottomed, non-reactive preserving pan with a lid ★ Wooden spoon ★ Timer ★ Bowl of hot water and a slotted spoon ★ Jam funnel if available, or ladle ★ Labels

1. Place some clean jam jars and their lids on a baking tray and then into the oven preheated to 100°C/200°F/Gas 2 for 20 minutes. Put two to three small plates or saucers in the freezer to chill. **2.** Wash the plums well in a colander, and leave to drain on a clean, ironed tea-towel. **3.** Cut the plums into halves or quarters, depending on size. As you do this remove the stones and discard them. **4.** Place the prepared fruit in a preserving pan and add the water. **5.** Place the pan over a moderate heat and cover with the lid. Bring up to a simmer and, stirring from time to time, cook the fruit until it has softened, about 10 minutes. **6.** Now turn the heat down to very low, remove the lid from the pan and add the sugar. Using a wooden spoon, stir the mixture until the sugar has completely dissolved. Make sure you cannot see any undissolved crystals of sugar on the sides of the pan and the back of the spoon. The jam should not feel gritty when stirred. **7.** Turn up the heat and bring the mixture to the boil. Cook the jam at a full rolling boil, one that can't be stirred down with the spoon, for 5 minutes, stirring quite often to stop the fruit catching on the bottom of the pan. **8.** Turn off the heat and make your first test for a set. Take a cold plate or saucer from the freezer and drop a spoonful of jam on to it. Leave for about 1 minute then push the side of the mixture gently with the tip of your finger and look at the surface. If it wrinkles, the jam is ready to pot. **9.** If the jam is still runny, turn the heat back on and boil for a further 2 minutes before testing again. Always turn off the heat while testing for a set. Repeat until the jam tests positive for a set. **10.** Once the jam has reached setting point, turn off the heat. Skim off any scum using a slotted spoon, rinsing it in a bowl of hot water between skims. **11.** Leave the jam to cool for 5 minutes. Take the baking tray of jars from the oven at the same time. **12.** Pot the jam into the hot jars. I use a jam funnel to help with this, but a ladle is fine. Top with the lids. **13.** When the jars are cold, label them, and check the lids are firmly screwed on. Store in a cool, dark place.

Raspberry Jam

No book I write will ever be without my recipe for raspberry jam. I feel it would be a tragedy for anyone not to make at least one jar of this simple and delicious jam. It is on my *Desert Island Discs* list of essentials and is the jam I make most often, believing as I do that it is best made in small quantities and eaten as fresh as possible.

Use ripe red raspberries, choosing one of the larger varieties if possible. If you are picking your own, try for a dry sunny day. Oh, and I often use thawed, frozen raspberries to make the jam, they work perfectly well.

Yield approx. 3 x 200ml | Keeps 6–9 months

500g raspberries
500g white granulated sugar

1 . Place some clean jam jars and their lids on a baking tray and then into the oven preheated to 100°C/200°F/Gas 2 for 20 minutes. Put two to three small plates or saucers in the freezer to chill. **2 .** Place the berries and sugar into a heavy-bottomed steel or enamelled pan and cook over a low heat until the fruit melts and the sugar is fully dissolved. Make sure you cannot see any undissolved crystals of sugar on the sides of the pan and the back of the spoon. The jam should not feel gritty when stirred. Don't worry that the berries break up. **3 .** Once the sugar has fully dissolved, turn up the heat and bring the mixture to the boil. Cook the jam at a full rolling boil, one that can't be stirred down with the spoon, for 5 minutes. **4 .** Turn off the heat and make your first test for a set. Take a cold plate or saucer from the freezer and drop a teaspoon of jam on to it. Leave for about a minute, then push the side of the mixture gently with your finger. If you can see the surface wrinkling your jam is ready to pot. **5 .** If the jam is still runny, turn the heat back on and boil for a further 2 minutes before testing again. Repeat the boil/testing process until the jam tests positive for a set. **6 .** Once the jam has reached setting point, turn off the heat. Skim off any scum that has collected on the top of the jam, using a slotted spoon, rinsing it in a bowl of hot water between skims. **7 .** Leave the jam to cool for 5 minutes. Take the baking tray of jars from the oven at the same time. **8 .** Pot the jam into the hot jars. I use a jam funnel to help with this, but a ladle is fine. Top with the lids. **9 .** When the jars are cold, label them, and check the lids are firmly screwed on. Store in a cool, dark place.

Apricot Jam

Apricot jam must be up there as another one of my favourites. There is a lushness about apricots that you don't find in other stone fruit: the flesh melts when they cook to give a rich texture without any real form.

Apricots are quite low in pectin unlike their cousins plums, and also, due to the sweetness of the flesh, low in acid, so both will have to be added along with sugar to give the perfect jam. Whilst the fruits are sweet this doesn't mean you can cut back on the added sugar if you want a perfectly set jam that keeps well.

You need to choose perfectly ripe apricots for this to maximise their heady perfume. Cut away any bruises and try not to use soft over-ripe fruit: you want to preserve only the best.

I simmer the fruit in some water to cook it before adding sugar, acid and pectin as this makes for a fresher tasting preserve.

Yield **approx. 1.3kg** | *Keeps* **6 months**

1kg apricots
200ml water
120ml fresh lemon juice
900g jam sugar

1 . Place some clean jam jars and their lids on a baking tray and then into the oven preheated to 100°C/200°F/Gas 2 for 20 minutes. Put two to three small plates or saucers in the freezer to chill. **2 .** Prepare the fruits by washing and draining them. Now cut them in half and remove and discard the stones. **3 .** Put the fruit and measured water into a heavy-bottomed pan and place on a low heat.

4 . Bring the contents of the pan to a simmer and cover with a lid. Cook for 15 minutes until the fruit is soft. **5 .** Now stir in the lemon juice and sugar and continue to cook over a low heat, stirring with a wooden spoon, until the sugar has completely dissolved. Make sure you cannot see any undissolved crystals of sugar on the sides of the pan and the back of the spoon. The jam should not feel gritty when stirred. **6 .** When the sugar has fully dissolved, turn up the heat and bring the mixture to the boil. Cook the jam at a full rolling boil, one that can't be stirred down with a spoon, for 4 minutes. Stir occasionally to prevent sticking. **7 .** Turn off the heat and make your first test for a set. Take a cold plate or saucer from the freezer and drop a spoonful of jam on to it. Leave for about 1 minute then push the side of the mixture gently with the tip of your finger and look at the surface. If it wrinkles the jam is ready to pot. **8 .** If the jam is still runny, turn the heat back on and boil for a further 2 minutes before testing again. Always turn off the heat while testing for a set. Repeat the boil/testing process until the jam tests positive for a set. **9 .** Once the jam has reached setting point, turn off the heat. Skim off any scum that has collected on the top of the jam, using a slotted spoon, rinsing it in a bowl of hot water between skims. **10 .** Leave the jam to cool for 5 minutes. Take the baking tray of jars from the oven at the same time. **11 .** Pot the jam into the hot jars. I use a jam funnel to help with this, but a ladle is fine. Top with the lids. **12 .** When the jars are cold, label them, and check the lids are firmly screwed on. Store in a cool, dark place.

Foragers' Jam

Anyone walking through the countryside in autumn will be delighted by the display of berries that brightens the hedgerows. The temptation to pick these has always been strong in me, but now it seems the whole world is out foraging.

Wild berries differ from their cultivated cousins, often being smaller, more tannic and much less sweet, all properties that are bred out of commercial varieties. These qualities need to be taken into consideration when using wild berries for preserves. Elderberries and wild blackberries also contain a high percentage of pips. To compensate for these disadvantages the flavour of these berries is more complex and makes for distinct and different preserves.

Yield **approx. 1kg** | *Keeps* **1 year**

400g wild blackberries, elderberries and sloes, mixed
600ml water
750g large crab or other sour apples, prepared weight
600g white granulated sugar
juice of 1 lemon

1. Place some clean jam jars and their lids on a baking tray and then into the oven preheated to 100°C/200°F/Gas 2 for 20 minutes. Put two to three small plates or saucers in the freezer to chill. **2.** Wash the berries well then put them and the water into a pan and cover with a lid. Place this on a medium heat and simmer the fruit until very soft and pulpy, about 15 minutes. **3.** Sieve the mixture into a clean bowl and then put this back into the cleaned pan. **4.** Peel, core and chop the apples and add to the pan. **5.** Place the pan on the heat and again cover the pan, simmering the mixture until the apple is soft, about 10 minutes. **6.** Now, off the heat, stir in the sugar and lemon juice, using a wooden spoon. Place the pan back on the heat and continue to stir often over a low heat until the sugar has fully dissolved. Make sure you cannot see any undissolved crystals of sugar on the sides of the pan and the back of the spoon. The jam should not feel gritty when stirred. **7.** Bring the mixture to the boil. Cook the jam at a full rolling boil, one that can't be stirred down with the spoon, for 5 minutes. Stir occasionally to stop the fruit from sticking to the pan. **8.** Turn off the heat and make your first test for a set. Take a cold plate or saucer from the freezer, and drop a small spoonful of jam on to it. Leave for about 1 minute then push the side of the mixture gently with the tip of your finger and look at the surface. If it wrinkles, the jam is ready to pot. **9.** If the jam is still runny, turn the heat back on and boil for a further 2 minutes before testing again. Always turn off the heat while testing for a set. Repeat the boil/testing process until the jam tests positive for a set. **10.** Once the jam has reached setting point, turn off the heat. Skim off any scum using a slotted spoon, rinsing it in a bowl of hot water between skims. **11.** Leave the jam to cool for 5 minutes. Take the baking tray of jars from the oven at the same time. **12.** Pot the jam into the hot jars. I use a jam funnel to help with this, but a ladle is fine. Top with the lids. **13.** When the jars are cold, label them, and check the lids are firmly screwed on. Store in a cool, dark place.

Black Cherry Jam

I love cherries. I love the colour, the subtle fragrance and the lushness of the fruit, all of which combine here to give a rich, luxurious preserve. Think scones (or even baguette slices) and cream, sourdough toast or crisp buttery waffles . . .

Cherries are stone fruit. They contain only small amounts of pectin and are also low in acid, so both these will need to be added. In common with blueberries and currants, cherry skins can be tough and ruin the texture of the jam, so the fruit must be simmered until soft before the sugar is added.

And, I'm afraid, the cherries will need stoning. I have an ancient cherry stoner that I use: you need to spread out a newspaper, as the juice gets everywhere, then put on the radio and get stoning.

If you can't get fresh cherries, or hate the idea of stoning them, you can use thawed frozen fruit which conveniently come ready stoned.

Yield **approx. 1.2kg** | *Keeps* **6 months**

1kg black or red cherries
200ml water
1kg jam sugar
100ml fresh lemon juice

1 . Place some clean jam jars and their lids on a baking tray and then into the oven preheated to 100°C/200°F/Gas 2 for 20 minutes. Put two to three small plates or saucers in the freezer to chill. **2 .** If you've chosen fresh cherries stone them over a pan or bowl to catch any juice. You may want to wear gloves, as the juice will stain your hands. **3 .** Put the cherries, their juices and the water into a pan: you can use your wide preserving pan if it has a lid. Bring to the boil, half cover with the lid, and simmer for 15 minutes. **4 .** Take the pan from the heat and stir in the sugar and lemon juice, using a wooden spoon. Put the pan on a low heat and stir until the sugar has completely dissolved. Make sure you cannot see any undissolved crystals of sugar on the sides of the pan and the back of the spoon. The jam should not feel gritty when stirred. **5 .** Now turn up the heat and bring the jam up to the boil. Cook at a full rolling boil, one that cannot be stirred down with the spoon, for 4 minutes. Stir from time to time to stop the fruit from sticking to the bottom of the pan. **6 .** Turn off the heat and make your first test for a set. Take a cold plate or saucer from the freezer and drop a spoonful of jam on to it. Leave for about a minute then push the side of the mixture gently with the tip of your finger and look at the surface. If it wrinkles, the jam is ready to pot. **7 .** If the jam is still runny, turn the heat back on and boil for a further 2 minutes before testing again. Always turn off the heat while testing for a set. Repeat the boil/testing process until the jam tests positive for a set. **8 .** Once the jam has reached setting point, turn off the heat. Skim off any scum that has collected on the top of the jam, using a slotted spoon, rinsing it in a bowl of hot water between skims. **9 .** Leave the jam to cool for 5 minutes. Take the baking tray of jars from the oven at the same time. **1 0 .** Pot the jam into the hot jars. I use a jam funnel to help with this, but a ladle is fine. Top with the lids. **1 1 .** When the jars are cold, label them, and check the lids are firmly screwed on. Store in a cool, dark place.

Gooseberry Jam

The good news here is that gooseberries make great jam: they are full of pectin and wonderfully acidic, so only need the addition of sugar. There are a couple of caveats though: gooseberry skins can be very tough if the fruit is not pre-cooked, and each berry needs to be topped and tailed by hand to remove the remains of the flower and the stem. This chore can't be left out, I'm afraid, but you could always enlist help, offering bribes of the finished jam.

Choose firm ripe fruit, avoiding any berries that are mouldy. Even if you pick green gooseberries, you will most likely have pink jam, the colour of the finished jam depending on the variety and ripeness of the berries.

Yield approx. 1.6kg | Keeps 6 months

1kg gooseberries
150ml water
1kg white granulated sugar

1 . Place some clean jam jars and their lids on a baking tray and then into the oven preheated to 100°C/200°F/Gas 2 for 20 minutes. Put two to three small plates or saucers in the freezer to chill. **2** . Begin by preparing the gooseberries. Using a small sharp knife, top and tail the fruit, discarding the tops and tails. Wash the gooseberries well. **3** . Place the fruit in a heavy-bottomed pan. Add the water, put the pan over a very low heat and cover with a lid. Bring the mixture up to a simmer and cook until the fruit is soft, about 5 minutes. Stir the pan once or twice to ensure all the berries are cooked. **4** . Take the pan from the heat and remove the lid. Stir in the sugar using a wooden spoon. Over a low heat, stirring gently, cook the jam until you can see and feel that the sugar has completely dissolved. Make sure you cannot see any undissolved crystals of sugar on the sides of the pan and the back of the spoon. The jam should not feel gritty when stirred. **5** . Turn up the heat and bring the jam to the boil. Cook the jam at a full rolling boil, one that cannot be stirred down with the spoon, for 4 minutes. Stir from time to time to stop the fruit from sticking to the bottom of the pan. **6** . Turn off the heat and make your first test for a set. Take a cold plate or saucer from the freezer and drop a spoonful of jam on to it. Leave for about 1 minute then push the side of the mixture gently with the tip of your finger and look at the surface. If it wrinkles, the jam is ready to pot. **7** . If the jam is still runny, turn the heat back on and boil for a further 2 minutes before testing again. Always turn off the heat while testing for a set. Repeat the boil/testing process until the jam tests positive for a set. **8** . Once the jam has reached setting point, turn off the heat. Skim off any scum that has collected on the top of the jam, using a slotted spoon, rinsing it in a bowl of hot water between skims. **9** . Leave the jam to cool for 5 minutes. Take the baking tray of jars from the oven at the same time. **10** . Pot the jam into the hot jars. I use a jam funnel to help with this, but a ladle is fine. Top with the lids. **11** . When the jars are cold, label them, and check the lids are firmly screwed on. Store in a cool, dark place.

Mixed Berry Jam

A simple recipe this, but a very useful one, as you can adapt it to whatever fruit you can find. If you're using gooseberries, rhubarb or blueberries, you will need to cook them a little first, then you can add the softer fruit such as strawberries, raspberries and currants.

I first made this when, after a woefully wet summer, I came in from the garden with a colander of fruit of many different varieties. I have since made it with a bag of frozen mixed red fruit, though I would avoid those that contain grapes.

If you are using a high proportion of strawberries, I would use jam sugar. Its added pectin will allow you to achieve a set with the minimum amount of boiling so that the wonderful fresh flavour of the fruit is caught in your jam.

Yield approx. 800–900g | *Keeps* 6 months

equal weight of fruit and jam sugar
juice of 1 large lemon per 500g fruit

1 . Place some clean jam jars and their lids on a baking tray and then into the oven preheated to 100°C/200°F/Gas 2 for 20 minutes. Put two to three small plates or saucers in the freezer to chill. **2 .** Prepare the fruit: chop rhubarb into 1cm pieces; top and tail gooseberries; pick over blueberries, removing any mouldy or squashed ones; cut large strawberries into halves and quarters; and de-string currants. **3 .** Wash the fruit gently under a running tap. Remember to keep harder fruits separate. **4 .** Put any rhubarb, gooseberries or blueberries into the preserving pan along with any water still clinging to the fruit, and place the pan, covered with a lid, over a low heat. **5 .** Cook this tougher fruit until it softens, about 5 minutes, then remove from the heat and add the rest of the berries, the sugar and lemon juice. **6 .** Cook gently over the same low heat, stirring with a wooden spoon, until the sugar has fully dissolved. Make sure you cannot see any undissolved crystals of sugar on the sides of the pan and the back of the spoon. The jam should not feel gritty when stirred. **7 .** Once the sugar has fully dissolved, turn up the heat and bring the mixture to the boil. Cook the jam at a full rolling boil, one that cannot be stirred down with the spoon, for 2 minutes. **8 .** Turn off the heat and make your first test for a set. Take a cold plate or saucer from the freezer and drop a spoonful of jam on to it. Leave for about 1 minute then push the side of the mixture gently with the tip of your finger and look at the surface. If it wrinkles, the jam is ready to pot. **9 .** If the jam is still runny, turn the heat back on and boil for a further 2 minutes before testing again. Always turn off the heat while testing for a set. Repeat the boil/testing process until the jam tests positive for a set. **1 0 .** Once the jam has reached setting point, turn off the heat. Skim off any scum that has collected on the top of the jam, using a slotted spoon, rinsing it in a bowl of hot water between skims. **1 1 .** Leave the jam to cool for about 5 minutes. Take the baking tray of jars from the oven at the same time. **1 2 .** Pot the jam into the hot jars. I use a jam funnel to help with this, but a ladle is fine. Top with the lids. **1 3 .** When the jars are cold, label them, and check the lids are firmly screwed on. Store in a cool, dark place.

Strawberry Balsamic Jam

Strawberry jam is one of the most difficult to make, and yet one we all long to eat. Strawberries, whilst one of the most wonderful and colourful summer fruits, are woefully low in pectin and acid, the two basic building blocks of jam making. Add to this the transient nature of the perfumed, fresh flavour of the berries, and you will see the difficulties.

To make the best strawberry jam, you need to use the sugaring technique described on page 19. To maximise your chances of success, make sure you buy good fruit. You need just ripe, small berries that are neither bruised nor crushed. Never buy 'Strawberries for Jam' as they are almost invariably over-ripe, poor-quality fruit that in turn will make awful jam. You will need to add both pectin and acid to the mix too, and the balsamic vinegar adds a wonderful extra layer of flavour.

Yield **approx. 1kg** | *Keeps* **6 months**

750g strawberries
750g jam sugar
juice of 1 large lemon
3 tablespoons balsamic vinegar

1 . Hull the strawberries, and if large cut in half or quarters. **2 .** Place the berries, sugar, lemon juice and vinegar in a large glass bowl and mix well with a spoon. **3 .** Now place this bowl in a warm place for 2 hours or overnight. The berries are ready when they have given up much of their juice. The sugar will have started to dissolve. **4 .** Place some clean jam jars and their lids on a baking tray and then into the oven preheated to 100°C/200°F/Gas 2 for 20 minutes. Put two to three small plates in the freezer to chill. **5 .** Now scrape everything from the bowl into a wide preserving or other heavy pan, and place this over a low heat. **6 .** Using a wooden spoon, stir the mixture until the sugar has completely dissolved. Make sure you cannot see any undissolved crystals of sugar on the sides of the pan and the back of the spoon. The jam should not feel gritty when stirred. **7 .** Once the sugar has fully dissolved, turn up the heat and bring the mixture to the boil. Cook the jam at a full rolling boil, one that can't be stirred down with the spoon, for 6 minutes, stirring quite often to stop the fruit catching on the bottom of the pan. **8 .** Turn off the heat and make your first test for a set. Take a cold plate from the freezer and drop a spoonful of jam on to it. Leave for about 1 minute then push the side of the mixture gently with the tip of your finger and look at the surface. If it wrinkles, the jam is ready to pot. **9 .** If the jam is still runny, turn the heat back on and boil for a further 2 minutes then switch off and test again. **10 .** Once the jam has reached setting point, turn off the heat. Skim off any scum using a slotted spoon, rinsing it in a bowl of hot water between skims. **11 .** Leave the jam to cool for about 5 minutes. Take the baking tray of jars from the oven at the same time. **12 .** Pot the jam into the hot jars. Top with the lids. **13 .** When the jars are cold, label them, and check the lids are firmly screwed on. Store in a cool, dark place.

Greengage Jam

I once owned a greengage tree that I had planted as part of a new orchard.

Greengages, I found, are notoriously awkward trees, fruiting when they choose, and not when you want them to. Five years after I planted the tree, I sold the house: I had never picked a single gage. The very next year the tree had so much fruit on it that one bough broke. You can't bend nature to your whim, and I now buy greengages from the market . . .

Greengages are smaller than many plums and make a luscious preserve. Like apricots, greengages are low in pectin so I add pectin by using jam sugar and a touch of lemon juice to add acid. Choose fresh ripe and firm fruit, avoiding any that are bruised or squashy.

Yield **approx. 1.2kg** | *Keeps* **6 months**

1kg greengages
200ml water
800g jam sugar
juice of 1 large lemon

1 . Place some clean jam jars and their lids on a baking tray and then into the oven preheated to 100°C/200°F/Gas 2 for 20 minutes. Put two to three small plates or saucers in the freezer to chill. **2 .** Begin by preparing the fruit. Wash and dry the greengages, then cut them into quarters, removing and discarding the stones. **3 .** Place the fruit and water into a preserving pan. Cover the pan with the lid, and put it over a low heat. **4 .** Cook the fruit, stirring from time to time, until the greengages begin to soften, about 10 minutes. **5 .** Now stir in the sugar and lemon juice and continue to cook over a low heat, stirring with a wooden spoon, until the sugar has completely dissolved. Make sure you cannot see any undissolved crystals of sugar on the sides of the pan and the back of the spoon. The jam should not feel gritty when stirred. **6 .** When the sugar has fully dissolved, turn up the heat and bring the jam to a boil. Cook the jam at a full rolling boil, one that can't be stirred down with the spoon, for 4 minutes. **7 .** Turn off the heat and make your first test for a set. Take a cold plate or saucer from the freezer and drop a spoonful of jam on to it. Leave for about 1 minute then push the side of the mixture gently with the tip of your finger and look at the surface. If it wrinkles the jam is ready to pot. **8 .** If the jam is still runny, turn the heat back on and boil for a further 2 minutes before testing again. Always turn off the heat while testing for a set. Repeat the boil/ testing process until the jam tests positive for a set. **9 .** Once the jam has reached setting point, turn off the heat. Skim off any scum that has collected on the top of the jam, using a slotted spoon, rinsing it in a bowl of hot water between skims. **10 .** Leave the jam to cool for 5 minutes. Take the baking tray of jars from the oven at the same time. **11 .** Pot the jam into the hot jars. I use a jam funnel to help with this, but a ladle is fine. Top with the lids. **12 .** When the jars are cold, label them, and check the lids are firmly screwed on. Store in a cool, dark place.

Banana & Lime Jam

I was just a little curious when a friend told me about this jam. I've heard of banana jams before and actually, if I'm honest, they really didn't appeal. But I value Catherine Phipps' opinions, and when she offered to share this with me for the book, I thought I'd give it a try.

I'm so glad I did, as it is delicious, not sickly sweet and not even with that rather artificial taste of cooked bananas, just a delicious, slightly chunky preserve that I will definitely make again.

You need ripe bananas, not black ones, but ones that are soft and sweet. As bananas contain pectin, you won't need to add any. Choose big fresh limes with good green skins, and scrub them well to remove any wax on the skin before making the jam.

Here the jam is started using the 'sugaring' method (see the Glossary, page 19). This is when the prepared fruit is mixed in advance with the sugar and left to sit for a given time.

Yield approx. 600g | *Keeps* 6 months

3 large limes
450g bananas, peeled weight (about 650g unpeeled)
280g white granulated sugar

1. Wash the limes well, scrubbing them with a scourer to remove any wax on the skin, then zest them, using a fine Microplane. Place the zest in a large glass bowl. **2.** Cut the limes in half and squeeze the juice into the bowl. **3.** Cut the bananas into small dice of about 5mm, and put them into the bowl. **4.** Sprinkle over the sugar, then mix well, tossing the fruit into the juice and sugar with a metal spoon. Cover the bowl and leave in a warm place for 2 hours or overnight.
5. Scrape the contents of the bowl into a heavy-bottomed saucepan and put this over a low heat. Stir often until the sugar has fully dissolved. Make sure you cannot see any undissolved crystals of sugar on the sides of the pan and the back of the spoon. The jam should not feel gritty when stirred. **6.** Cover the pan and cook at a low simmer for 45 minutes, stirring frequently to prevent the fruit from sticking to the bottom. **7.** Place some clean jam jars and their lids on a baking tray and then into the oven preheated to 100°C/200°F/Gas 2 for 20 minutes. Put two to three small plates or saucers in the freezer to chill. **8.** After 45 minutes take the lid from the pan and stir well. Remove the pan from the heat. **9.** Make your first test for a set. Take a cold plate or saucer from the freezer and put a small spoonful of jam on it. If it mounds when you push it with your finger, the jam is ready. **10.** If the jam runs across the plate, turn up the heat and boil the jam for 2 more minutes. **11.** Meanwhile, take the baking tray with the hot jars from the oven and allow to cool for 5 minutes. **12.** Pot the jam into the hot jars. I use a jam funnel to help with this, but a ladle is fine. Top with the lids. **13.** When the jars are cold, label them, and check the lids are firmly screwed on. Store in a cool, dark place.

Blueberry Jam

This should strictly be called blueberry and apple jam as I've added some apple purée to the mix to give a little body to the jam. The apple also helps with one other problem when making blueberry jam: the berries' woeful lack of pectin.

It is essential to cook the blueberries before you add the sugar to avoid the skins toughening up before the fruit cooks.

I serve this jam with yoghurt, crumpets or waffles.

Yield **approx. 1.2kg** | *Keeps* **6 months**

600g blueberries
250g Bramley apple, prepared weight (about 1 large apple)
100ml water
650g jam sugar

1 . Place some clean jam jars and their lids on a baking tray and then into the oven preheated to 100°C/200°F/Gas 2 for 20 minutes. Put two to three small plates or saucers in the freezer to chill. **2 .** Wash the blueberries and pick them over, removing any squashed or mouldy ones. **3 .** Peel and core the apple and chop it into small cubes. **4 .** Put the apple into the preserving pan with the water and place this over a low heat. Cover the pan and cook until the apple is a soft purée, about 5–10 minutes. **5 .** Now add the blueberries and return the pan to the heat. Cover with the lid, and simmer until the berries are soft, about 10 minutes. **6 .** Turn off the heat and stir in the sugar. Put the pan back on the heat and cook, stirring gently with a wooden spoon, until the sugar has completely dissolved. Make sure you cannot see any undissolved crystals of sugar on the sides of the pan and the back of the spoon. The jam should not feel gritty when stirred. **7 .** Once the sugar has dissolved, turn up the heat and bring the mixture to the boil. Cook the jam at a full rolling boil, one that can't be stirred down with the spoon, for 2 minutes. **8 .** Turn off the heat and make your first test for a set. Take a cold plate or saucer from the freezer and drop a spoonful of jam on to it. Leave for about 1 minute then push the side of the mixture gently with the tip of your finger and look at the surface. If it wrinkles, the jam is ready to pot. **9 .** If the jam is still runny, turn the heat back on and boil for a further 2 minutes before testing again. Always turn off the heat while testing for a set. Repeat the boil/testing process until the jam tests positive for a set. **10 .** Once the jam has reached setting point, turn off the heat. Skim off any scum that has collected on the top of the jam, using a slotted spoon, rinsing it in a bowl of hot water between skims. **11 .** Leave the jam to cool for 5 minutes. Take the baking tray of jars from the oven at the same time. **12 .** Pot the jam into the hot jars. I use a jam funnel to help with this, but a ladle is fine. Top with the lids. **13 .** When the jars are cold, label them, and check the lids are firmly screwed on. Store in a cool, dark place.

JELLIES

Perfect Jellies

To my mind jellies are the prettiest of all preserves. Jewel-bright in colour and with the faintest quiver when spooned from the jar, jellies are delicate, tender and, most importantly, delicious. Simple to make if the guidelines are followed, jellies can be both sweet and savoury. There is a lovely symmetry that comes with serving a herb-scented apple jelly with pork from pigs that have grazed in orchards, and offering pink spring lamb, its flavour redolent of the herbs the sheep have eaten, with a pure-tasting mint jelly.

Unlike jams, jellies are made from the strained juice of the fruit, which is cooked first, strained through a jelly bag, and the fruit pulp discarded.

Jellies can also be made from uncooked fruit juice, say pomegranate juice or orange juice, and on some occasions you can use wine.

Jelly making is particularly suitable when considering which preserve to make with either very pippy fruit, for instance blackberries, or with small stone fruit like damsons. The fruit needs little preparation before it is simmered in water, then all skins, pips and stones are caught in the bag as the juice drips through, a process which usually takes 10-12 hours.

Because you lose the pulp, and only use the juice, a jelly will invariably produce less end-product than a jam.

A FEW THINGS TO KNOW ABOUT MAKING JELLIES

The same balance of fruit, sugar, pectin and acid is needed for jellies as for jams and marmalades. Fruits that are high in pectin and acid are the best to use in jellies. But there is always something you can do to help along a fruit that might not set well: you could add some cooking apple to boost pectin; you could add some lemon juice to boost the acidity.

★ Choose good-quality fruit but here, if apples are bruised, the damaged parts can be cut away. Do avoid fruit that is squashed or mouldy.

★ You will need a large heavy-bottomed pan. This does not have to be a dedicated preserving pan but it must be non-reactive or acid-resistant.

★ If you are using a cloth, place it in a clean colander or sieve, and set this over a very deep bowl. The bottom of the colander must be above the dripped liquid.

★ To sterilise or scald the cloth, make sure first that it is clean. Place it in a saucepan, cover with water, and bring to the boil. Simmer for 5 minutes, then drain. You can also wash the cloth in a washing machine, then iron it with a hot iron, which will kill any lingering bacteria.

★ It is important not to squeeze the jelly bag or press the solids down in any way, as this will result in a cloudy preserve. Leave the fruit pulp to drip for at least 10–12 hours, or overnight.

★ Often, in making jellies, the weight of sugar used is dependent on the volume of juice produced by the dripping overnight. Generally speaking – although I have specified in most recipes – you usually need about 100g sugar per 100ml juice.

★ It is perfectly fine to re-use old jam jars and lids for jellies, but the jars must be spotlessly clean and not chipped or damaged. Any lids must be spotless too, with no sign of damage or rust.

★ I use white granulated sugar for its clean flavour and low cost. Raw sugars are not really suitable for jellies, but can be used should you wish for the richer colour and flavour they add.

★ When you add the sugar to the juice for a jelly, it is very important that you keep the pan over a low heat to make sure the sugar has dissolved fully before you bring the mixture up to a full rolling boil. This is because undissolved sugar may cause the jelly to crystallise and have an unpleasant texture. Timings involved in dissolving sugar will vary, according to sugar type, heat of liquid etc. But you can easily tell if the sugar has not dissolved: when you stir the jelly the sugar feels gritty against the sides of the pan and if you look at the back of the wooden spoon you are using you will see tiny grains of undissolved sugar.

★ As the jelly cooks it is advisable to brush the sides of the pan down occasionally with a pastry brush dipped in cold water. This cleans the pan and stops any jelly that has clung there from burning.

★ The same wrinkle test I use for jam works here too (see page 27).

★ Jellies tend to throw up more scum than jams, so have a slotted spoon ready to skim the surface once setting point is reached. Always rinse the spoon in hot water between skims. The important thing is not to stir the scum down into the mixture.

★ Jellies take well to added flavours so I often pop a cinnamon stick, some chilli flakes or even a star anise into pots of scalding jelly, after skimming, and before putting on their lids. You could also add herbs, flowers or seeds.

★ Sterilise your jars and lids by putting them on a baking tray in the oven preheated to 100ºC/200ºF/ Gas 2 to heat through, for at least 15 minutes. They should be hot when you pot your jellies.

★ I keep the jars on the baking tray to fill, and use a jam funnel. The funnel is not essential, a small ladle or a jug will do, but you really want to try and avoid getting the jars too messy.

★ As soon as you have potted the jelly, cover the jars with the lids. I use metal ones but you can use waxed paper and cellophane.

★ Once the jars have cooled, check the lids are screwed on tightly, and label the jars. You may think you'll remember what is in which, but take it from me you won't. Store the jelly, like other preserves, in a cool, dark cupboard or, if you have one, a pantry or larder.

How to Make the Perfect Jar of Crab Apple Jelly

Crab apples are the perfect fruit from which to make jellies. They are small, packed with that vital pectin and acid, and are really too tiny to peel and core or cook in any other way.

Yield approx. 1.kg | *Keeps* 6 months

Ingredients

1.5kg crab apples
1.2 litres water
approx. 1kg white granulated sugar
cinnamon sticks (optional)

Equipment

Measuring jug and scales ★ Colander ★ Chopping board and knife ★ Large heavy-bottomed, non-reactive preserving pan with a lid ★ Jelly bag and stand ★ Large clean glass or china bowl ★ Ladle ★ Some glass jars with lids, washed and dried ★ Baking tray ★ 2 small plates or saucers ★ Wooden spoon ★ Large metal slotted or skimming spoon, plus a small bowl of hot water ★ Metal teaspoon ★ Jam funnel or ladle ★ Labels

1. Wash the apples well and remove any leaves etc. Cut into halves if larger than a ping-pong ball. Place the prepared apples and water in a large pan. **2.** Place the pan, covered with a lid, over a moderate heat and cook, stirring occasionally, until the apples have collapsed and the mixture is soft, about 25 minutes. **3.** Set up your jelly bag in a place where it can remain undisturbed, placing the bowl underneath. Take the pan and set it close to the bag. Using a ladle spoon the mixture from the pan into the bag. **4.** Leave the bag alone, allowing the mixture to drip through for 10–12 hours. Do not squeeze the bag or your jelly will be cloudy. **5.** Put some clean jam jars and lids on a baking tray and then into the oven preheated to 100°C/200°F/Gas 2 for 20 minutes. Place a couple of small plates or saucers in the freezer to chill. **6.** Measure the liquid that you have in the bowl, and calculate how much sugar you will need: 500ml of juice needs 500g sugar. **7.** Pour the juice into the washed preserving pan and add the measured sugar. **8.** Place the pan over a low heat and warm the mixture, stirring often with a wooden spoon, until the sugar has fully dissolved. There should be no trace of grittiness in the pan or on the back of the spoon. **9.** Now bring the mixture up to the boil. Cook the jelly at a full rolling boil for 5 minutes. **10.** Turn off the heat and make your first test for a set. Take a cold plate or saucer from the freezer and spoon on a little jelly. Leave for a minute and then gently push the edge of the mixture. If the surface wrinkles the jelly is ready. **11.** If the jelly is still runny, return the pan to the heat and cook for a further 2 minutes before testing again. Always turn off the heat while testing for a set. **12.** Once you're happy the jelly will set, turn off the heat and skim off any scum using a slotted spoon, rinsing it in a bowl of hot water between skims. **13.** Leave the jelly to cool for 5 minutes. Take the baking tray of jars from the oven at the same time. **14.** Pot the jelly into the hot jars and drop in a cinnamon stick if using. Top with the lids. **15.** When the jars are cold, label them, and check the lids are firmly screwed on. Store in a cool, dark place.

Bergamot Jelly

The bergamot orange is a wonderfully fragrant citrus fruit that comes from Calabria in Italy. Bergamots are relatively new to the shops in the UK, but look out for them, they add quite delicious floral notes to your cooking. You may have tasted them in Earl Grey tea, bergamot oil from the rind adding the citrus note to this smoky blend.

I used my bergamots, adding Amalfi lemons, to make a lovely quivering pale lemon jelly that would be as good on crusty white bread as on sourdough toast.

Once the juice is back in the pan and the sugar has dissolved, you will find you need to cook this jelly for only 2–3 minutes to reach a set, so have everything ready before you start the final phase of cooking.

Yield **approx. 1.4kg** | *Keeps* **6 months**

2 bergamot oranges
2 large Amalfi lemons
1 litre water
1kg white granulated sugar

1 . Scrub the fruit well in hot water first, and then chop roughly. **2 .** Put the chopped fruit into a food processor and whizz until finely chopped. **3 .** Scrape the fruit into a large heavy-bottomed, non-reactive pan and pour in the water. **4 .** Put the pan over a medium heat, cover with a lid and bring to the boil. Simmer for 30 minutes. **5 .** Set up your jelly bag in a place where it can remain undisturbed, placing a large bowl underneath. Take the pan and set it close to the bag. Using a ladle spoon the mixture from the pan into the bag.

6 . Leave the bag alone, allowing the mixture to drip through for 10–12 hours. Do not squeeze the bag or your jelly will be cloudy. **7 .** Put some clean jam jars and lids on a baking tray and then into the oven preheated to 100°C/200°F/Gas 2 for 20 minutes. Place two to three small plates or saucers in the freezer to chill. **8 .** Measure the juice in the bowl: you should have about a litre. If not, add enough water to bring it up to a litre. **9 .** Pour this into the washed preserving pan. Add the sugar and stir over a low heat until the sugar has fully dissolved. There should be no trace of grittiness in the pan or on the back of the spoon. **10 .** Now bring the mixture up to the boil. Cook the jelly at a full rolling boil, one that can't be stirred down with the spoon, for 2 minutes only. **11 .** Turn off the heat and make your first test for a set. Take a cold plate or saucer from the freezer and spoon on a little jelly. Leave for a minute and then gently push the edge of the mixture. If the surface wrinkles the jelly is ready. **12 .** If the jelly is still runny, return the pan to the heat and cook for a further 2 minutes before testing again. Always turn off the heat while testing for a set. **13 .** Once you are happy the jelly will set, turn off the heat and skim off any scum with a slotted spoon, rinsing it in a bowl of hot water between skims. **14 .** Now leave the jelly to cool for 5 minutes. Take the baking tray of jars from the oven at the same time. **15 .** Pot the jelly into the hot jars. I use a jam funnel to help with this, but a ladle is fine. Top with the lids. **16 .** When the jars are cold, label them, and check the lids are firmly screwed on. Store in a cool, dark place.

A Jelly of Strawberries & Roses

Wine jellies are delicious and can be made quite easily using a variety of wines, red, white and rosé. Pretty as a picture, this one is a fragrant blend of pink wine and strawberries, a summer treat if ever I saw one. Or perhaps the best Valentine's Day breakfast ever.

Yield **approx.** 1kg | *Keeps* 6 months

500g ripe strawberries
1 x 750ml bottle rosé wine
700g jam sugar
1 teaspoon citric acid powder
2 tablespoons rosewater
4 tablespoons dried Persian rose petals

1 . Begin by preparing the fruit. Remove the stems and then wash the berries, shaking the water from them. **2 .** Put the berries into a blender or food processor. Whizz until you have a purée. **3 .** Pour the wine into a heavy-bottomed saucepan and add the strawberry purée. Warm the mixture over a low heat for about 3–4 minutes, then leave to infuse for 1 hour. **4 .** Set up your jelly bag in a place where it can remain undisturbed, placing a large bowl underneath. Take the pan and set it close to the bag. Using a ladle spoon the mixture from the pan into the bag. **5 .** Leave the bag alone, allowing the mixture to drip through for 10–12 hours. Do not squeeze the bag or your jelly will be cloudy. **6 .** Put some clean jam jars and lids on a baking tray and then into the oven preheated to 100°C/200°F/Gas 2 for 20 minutes. Place a couple of small plates or saucers in the freezer to chill. **7 .** Pour the juice into a clean pan and add the sugar and citric acid. **8 .** Place this over a low heat and cook gently, stirring until the sugar has fully dissolved. There should be no trace of grittiness in the pan or on the back of the spoon. **9 .** Now bring the mixture up to a boil. Cook the jelly at a full rolling boil, one that can't be stirred down with the spoon, for 5 minutes. **10 .** Turn off the heat, and make your first test for a set. Take a cold plate or saucer from the freezer and spoon on a little jelly. Leave for a minute, to allow the jelly to cool slightly, and then gently push the edge of the mixture. If the surface wrinkles the jelly is ready. **11 .** If the jelly is still runny, return the pan to the heat and cook for a further 2 minutes before testing again. Always turn off the heat while testing for a set. **12 .** Once you are happy the jelly will set, turn off the heat and skim off any scum with a slotted spoon, rinsing it in a bowl of hot water between skims. **13 .** Once this is done, stir in the rosewater and the rose petals, and allow the jelly to sit for 10 minutes. **14 .** Stir again, then place the pan back on the heat and bring gently up to boiling point. **15 .** Take the pan from the heat and leave for 5 minutes. Take the baking tray of jars from the oven at the same time. **16 .** Pot the jelly into the hot jars and top with the lids. **17 .** When the jars are cold, label them, and check the lids are firmly screwed on. The rose petals will float to the top and look so pretty. Store in a cool, dark place.

Hot Chilli Jelly

So simple to make, this chilli jelly recipe can be easily adapted to suit your individual tastes. I sometimes add lemongrass and lime zest to give it a Thai slant, or stir in a spoonful of smoked paprika for a Spanish flavour.

I like to leave the pepper flesh in the mix, but it can be sieved out should you want a clear jelly.

Yield **approx. 1.6kg for jelly with pepper pulp**
1.2kg for jelly with pulp sieved out
Keeps **6 months**

600g red peppers, prepared weight (about 3 large peppers)
6–10 fresh, hot, red chillies
350ml white or red wine vinegar
1kg jam sugar

1 . Start by preparing the vegetables. Cut the peppers and chillies in half and remove all the seeds, pith and stalks. **2 .** Put the prepared flesh in a food processor and blitz until you have a finely chopped mix. **3 .** Scrape this into a heavy-bottomed saucepan and pour in the vinegar. **4 .** Cover with the lid, place the pan over a low heat and bring the contents up to a simmer. Take the lid off and cook, uncovered, for 5 minutes. **5 .** Now, if you want to make a clear jelly, set up your jelly bag in a place where it can remain undisturbed, placing a large bowl underneath. Take the pan and set it close to the bag. Using a ladle spoon the mixture from the pan into the bag. Leave the bag alone, allowing the mixture to drip through for 10–12 hours. Do not squeeze the bag or your jelly will be cloudy. **6 .** Or, if you want to retain the pepper pulp in the jelly, simply continue with the recipe. **7 .** Put some clean jam jars and lids on a baking tray and then into the oven preheated to 100°C/200°F/Gas 2 to heat through gently. Place two to three small plates or saucers in the freezer to chill. **8 .** Either measure the juice that has dripped overnight and add 100g sugar for each 100ml, or add all the sugar to the softened pepper pulp in the pan. **9 .** Put the pan over a low heat and stir until the sugar has fully dissolved. There should be no trace of grittiness in the pan or on the back of the spoon. **10 .** Now bring the mixture up to the boil. Cook the jelly at a full rolling boil, one that can't be stirred down with the spoon, for 5 minutes. **11 .** Turn off the heat and make your first test for a set. Take a cold plate or saucer from the freezer and spoon on a little jelly. Leave for a minute and then gently push the edge of the mixture. If the surface wrinkles the jelly is ready. **12 .** If the jelly is still runny, return the pan to the heat and cook for a further 2 minutes before testing again. Always turn off the heat while testing for a set. The jelly should only cook for between 6 and 8 minutes. **13 .** Once you are happy your jelly will set, turn off the heat and skim off any scum with a slotted spoon, rinsing it in a bowl of hot water between skims. **14 .** Once this is done, stir in any additional flavours, then let the jelly sit for about 5 minutes. Take the baking tray of jars from the oven at the same time. **15 .** Pot the jelly into the hot jars. I use a jam funnel to help with this, but a ladle is fine. Top with the lids. **16 .** When the jars are cold, label them, and check the lids are firmly screwed on. Store in a cool, dark place.

Damson Jelly with Chilli, Juniper & Rosemary

Damsons are small, full of pips and usually crop prolifically, but what to do with them? This jelly deals well with the masses of small stones and skin to flesh ratio.

Yield **approx. 600g** | *Keeps* **6 months**

750g damsons
300ml water
2 sprigs fresh rosemary
2 teaspoons juniper berries
2 fresh red chillies or 1 teaspoon dried chilli flakes
300g white granulated sugar
1 teaspoon juniper berries
1 sprig fresh rosemary
½ teaspoon dried chilli flakes

1 . Begin by washing the damsons then place them in a heavy-bottomed pan with the water. **2 .** Chop the rosemary, juniper berries and fresh chillies roughly, and put these into the pan too. **3 .** Place the pan over a moderate heat, cover and bring to a simmer. Cook the damsons for 20–30 minutes or until very soft. **4 .** Mash the mixture with a potato masher, then leave everything to infuse for 2–3 hours. **5 .** When you are ready, set up your jelly bag in a place where it can remain undisturbed, placing a large bowl underneath. Take the pan and set it close to the bag. Using a ladle spoon the mixture from the pan into the bag. **6 .** Leave the bag alone, allowing the mixture to drip through for 10–12 hours. Do not squeeze the bag or your jelly will be cloudy. **7 .** Put some clean jam jars and lids on a baking tray and then into the oven preheated to 100°C/200°F/Gas 2 for 20 minutes. Place two to three small plates or saucers in the freezer to chill. **8 .** Measure the juice into the clean pan, making it up to 400ml with water if necessary. **9 .** Add the sugar and place the pan over a low heat, stirring until the sugar has fully dissolved. There should be no trace of grittiness in the pan or on the back of the spoon. **10 .** Now bring the mixture up to the boil. Cook the jelly at a full rolling boil for 6 minutes. **11 .** Turn off the heat and make your first test for a set. Take a cold plate or saucer from the freezer and spoon on a little jelly. Leave for a minute and then gently push the edge of the mixture. If the surface wrinkles the jelly is ready. **12 .** If the jelly is still runny, return the pan to the heat and cook for a further 2 minutes before testing again. The jelly should only cook for between 7 and 10 minutes. **13 .** Once you are happy the jelly will set, turn off the heat and skim off any scum with a slotted spoon, rinsing it in a bowl of hot water between skims. **14 .** Once this is done, finely chop the juniper berries and rosemary and mix these into the jelly along with the chilli flakes. **15 .** Return the jelly to the heat, and bring just to boiling point. Turn off the heat, then allow the jelly to cool for 5 minutes. Take the baking tray of jars from the oven at the same time. **16 .** Pot the jelly into the hot jars and top with the lids. **17 .** When the jars are cold, label them, and check the lids are firmly screwed on. Store in a cool, dark place.

Redcurrant (Blackcurrant or even Whitecurrant) Jelly

Red-, black- and whitecurrants are one of the earliest fruits in the garden. Sharp, acidic and a bird magnet, I think the best way to preserve these rather old-fashioned fruits is to make a jelly or cordial.

Redcurrant jelly is a traditional accompaniment to English lamb dishes: it is less assertive than mint and has the necessary bite to cut through the fatty meat. Potted into small jars, the jelly can be made with a mixture of currants if the birds beat you to the bushes! This recipe can be doubled or tripled easily if you have a large crop of currants.

Yield **approx. 300g** | *Keeps* **6 months**

500g currants
250ml water
approx. 500g white granulated sugar

1. Pick the fruit over, removing any squashed or mouldy currants, then rinse in a colander under a running tap. **2.** Shake off the excess water and put the currants into a heavy-bottomed saucepan. Add the water. **3.** Cover the pan with a lid and bring the contents up to a simmer, cooking for 30 minutes. **4.** Using a fork or potato masher, mash the fruit to a rough purée. **5.** Set up your jelly bag in a place where it can remain undisturbed, placing a large bowl underneath. Take the pan and set it close to the bag. Using a ladle spoon the mixture from the pan into the bag. **6.** Leave the bag alone, allowing the mixture to drip through for 10–12 hours. Do not squeeze the bag or your jelly will be cloudy. **7.** Place some clean jam jars and lids on a baking tray and then into the oven preheated to 100°C/200°F/Gas 2 for 20 minutes. Place two to three small plates or saucers in the freezer to chill. **8.** Measure the juice that has collected. You need 100g sugar for each 100ml juice. **9.** Put the juice and sugar into a clean pan and place this over a low heat. Stirring often, cook gently until the sugar has fully dissolved. There should be no trace of grittiness in the pan or on the back of the spoon. **10.** Now bring the mixture up to the boil. Cook the jelly at a full rolling boil, one that can't be stirred down with the spoon, for 3 minutes. **11.** Turn off the heat and make your first test for a set. Take a cold plate or saucer from the freezer and spoon on a little jelly. Leave for a minute and then gently push the edge of the mixture. If the surface wrinkles, the jelly is ready. **12.** If the jelly is still runny, return the pan to the heat and cook for a further 2 minutes before testing again. The jelly should only cook for between 6 and 8 minutes. **13.** Once you are happy the jelly will set, turn off the heat and skim off any scum with a slotted spoon, rinsing it in a bowl of hot water between skims. **14.** Once this is done, let the jelly cool for about 5 minutes. Take the baking tray of jars from the oven at the same time. **15.** Pot the jelly into the hot jars. I use a jam funnel to help with this, but a ladle is fine. Top with the lids. **16.** When the jars are cold, label them, and check the lids are firmly screwed on. Store in a cool, dark place.

Quince Jelly with Cardamom & Vanilla

This may well be one of the prettiest preserves you ever make. Quinces, though yellowish in colour as a fruit, yield a wonderful pale pink juice that easily sets, quince being rich in pectin, into a lovely iridescent jelly.

As can sometimes happen with pretty things, quince juice is rather bland and boring, but that said it does act as the perfect carrier for other flavours, and here I've used crushed cardamom and vanilla seeds. These two work well together, and by adding the seeds once setting point is reached, you will have jars of jewel-like jelly with the spices suspended in them.

Quince does take a long boil to soften, so if you have a pressure cooker now is the time to get it out. Otherwise just boil, at a slow simmer, for 60 minutes or so until the quinces collapse into a pulp.

Choose firm ripe fruits, cutting away any bruised or damaged flesh. I prefer not to use fruit that has patches of mould as this can taint the finished preserve.

Yield **approx. 1.2kg |** *Keeps* **6 months**

1.4kg fresh quinces
1 litre water
1 teaspoon citric acid powder
900g white granulated sugar
20 cardamom pods
1 vanilla pod

1 . Wash the fruit well and cut into large pieces. **2 .** Place the fruit and the water in either a pressure cooker or a heavy-bottomed saucepan with a lid, and put over a moderate heat. **3 .** Cook the fruit for 12 minutes at high pressure if using a pressure cooker, allowing the pan to come down to room pressure slowly. If using an ordinary saucepan simmer, covered, until the fruit collapses, about 45–60 minutes. **4 .** Once the fruit is cooked, mash it well with a potato masher. **5 .** Set up your jelly bag in a place where it can remain undisturbed, placing a large bowl underneath. Take the pan and set it close to the bag. Using a ladle spoon the mixture from the pan into the bag. **6 .** Leave the bag alone, allowing the mixture to drip through for 10–12 hours. Do not squeeze the bag or your jelly will be cloudy. **7 .** Put some clean jam jars and lids on a baking tray and then into the oven preheated to 100°C/200°F/Gas 2 for 20 minutes. Place two to three small plates or saucers in the freezer to chill. **8 .** Measure the juice, making it up to 1 litre with water if necessary, and place this in a heavy pan. Stir the citric acid and sugar into the juice and place the pan over a low heat. **9 .** Cook the mixture gently, stirring often, until the sugar has completely dissolved. There should be no trace of grittiness in the pan or on the back of the spoon. **1 0 .** Now bring the mixture up to the boil. Cook the jelly at a full rolling boil, one that can't be stirred down with the spoon, for 5 minutes. **1 1 .** While the mixture boils, prepare the spices. Crush the cardamom pods and take out the black seeds, discarding the green pods. Now crush the seeds to release the wonderful perfume. Split the vanilla pod open with a small sharp knife and scrape out the seeds. Keep these ready for later. **1 2 .** After 5 minutes turn off the heat, and make your first test for a set. Take a cold plate or saucer from the freezer and spoon on a little jelly.

Leave for a minute and then gently push the edge of the mixture. If the surface wrinkles the jelly is ready. **13.** If the jelly is still runny, return the pan to the heat and cook for a further 2 minutes before testing again. Always turn off the heat when testing for a set. The jelly should only cook for between 6 and 8 minutes. **14.** Once you are happy the jelly will set, turn off the heat and skim off any scum with a slotted spoon, rinsing it in a bowl of hot water between skims. **15.** Once this is done, stir in the cardamom and vanilla seeds, then let the jelly cool for about 5 minutes. Take the baking tray of jars from the oven at the same time. **16.** Pot the jelly into the hot jars. I use a jam funnel to help with this, but a ladle is fine. Top with the lids. **17.** When the jars are cold, label them, and check the lids are firmly screwed on. Store in a cool, dark place.

Herb Jellies

You can use a wide variety of herbs to make these jellies, using the same apple base. More robust herbs work best – such as rosemary, bay, sage and thyme – but basil and mint will work well too. Potted in small jars, these herb jellies make lovely gifts.

Any sour or cooking apples will work well and you can use windfalls as long as you cut away any bruised areas.

Yield **approx. 1kg** | *Keeps* **6 months**

1.5kg Bramley or similar cooking apples
1 litre water
a large handful of fresh herbs
approx. 1kg white granulated sugar
100ml cider vinegar

1 . First prepare the apples. Wash the fruit under running water then chop roughly, cutting away any bruised parts. **2 .** Place the apples and the water in a heavy pan, cover with a lid and bring the contents up to boiling point. Simmer for 30 minutes or until the apples are very soft. **3 .** Set up your jelly bag in a place where it can remain undisturbed, placing a large bowl underneath. Take the pan and set it close to the bag. Using a ladle spoon the mixture from the pan into the bag. **4 .** Leave the bag alone, allowing the mixture to drip through for 10–12 hours. Do not squeeze the bag or your jelly will be cloudy. **5 .** Put some clean jam jars and lids on a baking tray and then into the oven preheated to 100°C/200°F/Gas 2 for 20 minutes. Place a couple of small plates or saucers in the freezer to chill. **6 .** Prepare the herbs, by washing them under running cold water,

and leaving to dry on a tea-towel. Strip away and discard any tough stems. Chop the leaves finely. You need about 3–4 tablespoons. **7 .** Measure the juice, allowing 500g sugar to each 500ml juice. **8 .** Put the juice, the correct amount of sugar and the vinegar into a heavy-bottomed pan. **9 .** Place the pan over a low heat and cook gently, stirring from time to time until the sugar has completely dissolved. There should be no trace of grittiness in the pan or on the back of the spoon. **10 .** Now bring the mixture up to the boil. Cook the jelly at a full rolling boil, one that can't be stirred down with the spoon, for 5 minutes. **11 .** Turn off the heat and make your first test for a set. Take a cold plate or saucer from the freezer and spoon on a little jelly. Leave for a minute and then gently push the edge of the mixture. If the surface wrinkles the jelly is ready. **12 .** If the jelly is still runny, return the pan to the heat and cook for a further 2 minutes before testing again. **13 .** Once you are happy the jelly will set, turn off the heat and skim off any scum with a slotted spoon, rinsing it in a bowl of hot water between skims. **14 .** Now stir in the chopped herbs, and bring the jelly back to boiling point. Turn off the heat. **15 .** Leave the jelly to cool for 5 minutes. Take the baking tray of jars from the oven at the same time. **16 .** Pot the jelly into the hot jars. If you like, pop a small sprig of the same herb into the jelly, then top with the lids. **17 .** When the jars are cold, label them, and check the lids are firmly screwed on. Store in a cool, dark place.

Sloe Gin & Ginger Jelly

If you make sloe gin, once you've bottled the gin, you will have some still usable sloes left. I like to make jelly with these as it seems wasteful just to throw them out. If you just have extra sloes, this will work too!

Sloes have a somewhat bitter, slightly tannic flavour, and this works well with spices such as ginger or anise. Juniper and rosemary would also work well here.

Yield approx. 600g | *Keeps* 1 year

500g fresh or reserved sloes
60g fresh root ginger, finely chopped
500ml water

For each 500ml juice
45ml fresh lemon juice
500g jam sugar
75ml sloe gin

1 . Place the sloes, ginger and water in a pan, bring up to a simmer then cover the pan with a lid and cook for 45 minutes. **2 .** Set up your jelly bag in a place where it can remain undisturbed, placing a large bowl underneath. Take the pan and set it close to the bag. Using a ladle spoon the mixture from the pan into the bag. **3 .** Leave the bag alone, allowing the mixture to drip through for 10–12 hours. Do not squeeze the bag or your jelly will be cloudy. **4 .** Put some clean jam jars and lids on a baking tray and then into the oven preheated to 100°C/200°F/Gas 2 for 20 minutes. Place two to three small plates or saucers in the freezer to chill. **5 .** Measure the juice and pour into a deep heavy saucepan. For each 500ml juice add 500g sugar to the pan along with 45ml lemon juice. **6 .** Cook the mixture over a low heat, stirring often, until the sugar has fully dissolved. There should be no trace of grittiness in the pan or visible on the back of the spoon. **7 .** Bring the mixture up to the boil and cook the jelly at a full rolling boil, one that cannot be stirred down with the spoon, for 4 minutes. **8 .** Turn off the heat and make your first test for a set. Take a cold plate or saucer from the freezer and spoon on a little jelly. Leave for a minute and then gently push the edge of the mixture. If the surface wrinkles the jelly is ready. **1 0 .** If the jelly is still runny, return the pan to the heat and cook for a further 2 minutes before testing again. **1 1 .** Once you are happy the jelly will set, turn off the heat and skim off any scum with a slotted spoon, rinsing it in a bowl of hot water between skims. **1 2 .** Once this is done, stir in the sloe gin. Allow the jelly to cool for about 5 minutes. Take the baking tray of jars from the oven at the same time. **1 3 .** Pot the jelly into the hot jars. I use a jam funnel to help with this, but a ladle is fine. Top with the lids. **1 4 .** When the jars are cold, label them, and check the lids are firmly screwed on. Store in a cool, dark place.

Bramble Jelly

Wild blackberries can often be small, and so the ratio of pips to flesh can make them unsuitable for use in jams. Bramble jelly is the answer, the complex flavour of the wild fruit making for a more interesting tea-time treat than their tame cousins.

Superstition states that you must pick your blackberries before Hallowe'en or the witches will have spat on them. I think this has more to do with the fruit becoming dry or mouldy, but you have been warned . . .

Yield **approx. 1.2kg** | *Keeps* **6 months**

1kg blackberries
2 large whole cooking apples, about 450g
500ml water
white granulated sugar

1 . Begin by preparing the fruit. Pick over the berries, discarding any mouldy ones. Chop the apples, peel, core and all, into rough cubes. **2 .** Put the apple, berries and the water into a heavy-bottomed pan. Cover the pan with the lid and place over a medium heat. **3 .** Bring the contents of the pan to a simmer, then cook the fruit until very soft, about 15 minutes. The apple must have broken down completely. **4 .** Set up your jelly bag in a place where it can remain undisturbed, placing a large bowl underneath. Take the pan and set it close to the bag. Using a ladle spoon the mixture from the pan into the bag. **5 .** Leave the bag alone, allowing the mixture to drip through for 10–12 hours. Do not squeeze the bag or your jelly will be cloudy. **6 .** Put some clean jam jars and lids on a baking tray and then into the oven preheated to 100°C/200°F/Gas 2 for 20 minutes. Place two to three small plates or saucers in the freezer to chill. **7 .** Measure the juice into the clean pan and add the correct weight of sugar – 100g per 100ml juice. **8 .** Place the pan over a low heat and cook gently, stirring until the sugar has fully dissolved. There should be no trace of grittiness in the pan or on the back of the spoon. **9 .** Now bring the mixture up to the boil. Cook the jelly at a full rolling boil, one that can't be stirred down with the spoon, for 3 minutes. **10 .** Turn off the heat and make your first test for a set. Take a cold plate or saucer from the freezer and spoon on a little jelly. Leave for a minute and then gently push the edge of the mixture. If the surface wrinkles the jelly is ready. **11 .** If the jelly is still runny, return the pan to the heat and cook for a further 2 minutes before testing again. The jelly should only cook for between 6 and 8 minutes. **12 .** Once you are happy the jelly will set, turn off the heat and skim off any scum with a slotted spoon, rinsing it in a bowl of hot water between skims. **13 .** Now leave the jelly to cool for 5 minutes. Take the baking tray of jars from the oven at the same time. **14 .** Pot the jelly into the hot jars. I use a jam funnel to help with this, but a ladle is fine. Top with the lids. **15 .** When the jars are cold, label them, and check the lids are firmly screwed on. Store in a cool, dark place.

FRUIT
CURDS

Perfect Fruit Curds

Curds are elegant sweet preserves, containing butter and eggs, which are best made in small quantities and stored in the fridge. They have a smooth velvety texture, and a richness that makes them an ideal filling for sponge cakes, a topping for meringues or a breakfast treat. I sometimes speculate as to why fruit curds are so called. The very last thing you want to see in the pan are actual curds; these usually mean the mix has boiled and you have a pan of sweet scrambled egg.

Don't let the fact that this is an exact technique put you off making these curds. Once you get the hang of things you will want to experiment with all kinds of flavours. The basics are simple. You just use fruit juice, eggs, sugar and butter or sometimes cream.

A FEW THINGS TO KNOW ABOUT MAKING FRUIT CURDS

★ When you have chosen your fruit, you need to prepare your juice. Sometimes this is as simple as squeezing lemons, oranges or limes, but sometimes you will need to cook the fruit and then strain out the juice. I tend not to use fruit purées as they give a denser texture to the curd, but you could try using a sieved purée.

★ If you are making a citrus curd, you will want to use the flavour locked in the zest. And so you will need to give the skin of the fruit a good scrub using a vegetable brush or scourer plus hot water to get rid of any wax coating. Then you should use your finest grater to collect all the zest from the skin, leaving the bitter white pith behind. I like to use a Microplane.

★ Use fresh free-range eggs and beat them enough to make them liquid. I then sieve my eggs to remove any lumps of albumen. In the recipes I have listed eggs by shelled weight to allow you to use whatever you usually buy.

★ Butter should be at room temperature and cut into small, 1cm, cubes so it melts quickly. I use salted butter as I prefer the depth of flavour that trace of salt gives. Remember the butter is one of the constituent flavours, so mild creamy butter will give a milder taste to your curd, and of course you could use unsalted butter.

★ Curds need to be stored in the fridge, so those made with butter will have a slightly granular texture when eaten very cold. However, those made with double cream do not share this problem. The cream gives a smooth texture to the finished curd, even when eaten straight from the fridge. I particularly like to eat curds made with cream with desserts like meringues.

★ I use white caster sugar to make curds, as it dissolves easily and is simply sweet, giving no other flavour to the curd. To my mind this is not the place for the bullying flavours of raw sugar. Although caster sugar dissolves more easily than granulated, it is still difficult to specify timings: you must always check that the pan no longer feels gritty, and that there are no signs of sugar crystals on your wooden spoon before continuing with the recipe.

★ I cook the curds in a deep, heavy, flat-bottomed frying pan made of hard anodised aluminium or a wide, deep sauté pan. You are looking for a heavy-bottomed pan that is 10cm or so deep and 20–30cm wide, which will give a good surface area for the curd to cook. Pans with very upright sides are fine so long as you make sure you stir every part of the base as the mixture can stick and may burn.

★ It is essential that you stir the curd constantly as it cooks, using a wooden spoon. To begin with, this mixes the curd together, then once you have a smooth mixture, the stirring ensures even cooking, which will give you the requisite thick, velvety texture. You should stir in a zig-zag motion, making sure you reach every part of the bottom of the pan. This is essential, again to make sure the curd cooks evenly: the centre can overheat whilst the sides of the pan are still cool.

★ Curds are cooked over a very low heat and you must never leave the pan unattended as the mixture can boil in seconds.

★ The important thing to remember here is that this cooking will take time. You could be stirring for at least 10 minutes. The consistency you are looking for is one that coats the back of your spoon. To test this turn the spoon over and run your finger across the back of the bowl. If you can see a clean line the curd is nearly ready.

★ If you see signs that the curd is about to boil, take the pan from the heat at once. If there is only a slight bubble, you can usually stir this in. If the mixture has stuck to the bottom of the pan, or you can see tiny bits of scrambled egg, then tip the mixture immediately into a clean bowl. The important thing is to get the curd out of the hot pan as soon as possible. Once you've done that, wash your pan, sieve the curd back into it, and reheat before potting, or carry on cooking if the saved curd is not thick enough.

★ I have seen recipes for curds using cornflour as a thickening agent. This is really not necessary, and will give a thick cloying texture to the curd. Simply cook the curd over a low heat, stirring constantly until it thickens.

★ Curds need spotlessly clean sterilised jars. Small jars are best here. I use small glass yoghurt pots, covering them with waxed discs and cellophane seals, or 200g jam jars with metal lids. Wash the jars and lids in hot soapy water, and then dry. Put them on a baking tray and into the oven preheated to 100°C/200°F/Gas 2. Leave for 15-20 minutes, then remove from the oven and rest for 5 minutes before potting the curd.

★ Once you have covered them, store your jars of curds in the fridge. They will keep for up to six weeks.

How to Make the Perfect Jar of Lemon Curd

As the zest is an important part of this curd, choose large, perfect-skinned, bright yellow lemons. They should feel heavy in your hand, which shows they are full of juice. If you can get unwaxed Amalfi lemons, so much the better.

Yield approx. 800g | *Keeps* 3–4 weeks in the fridge

Ingredients
4 large lemons
250g fresh eggs
150g salted butter
200g caster sugar

Equipment
Measuring jug and scale ★ Vegetable brush or scourer ★ Microplane or other fine grater ★ Chopping board and sharp knife ★ Bowl and whisk ★ Sieve ★ Large heavy, flat-bottomed pan ★ Some glass jars with lids, washed and dried ★ Baking tray ★ Wooden spoon ★ Timer ★ Jam funnel and metal spoon or ladle ★ Labels

1. Begin by washing the lemons in hot water to remove any dust or dirt. Scrub them with a brush or scourer to remove any dirt or wax. **2.** Using a Microplane or other fine grater, zest the lemons into a bowl. Cut in half and squeeze out all the juice into the bowl along with the zest. **3.** Whisk the weighed eggs lightly until smooth, and sieve them into your heavy-bottomed pan. **4.** Chop the butter into 1cm cubes and put into the pan with the eggs. Add the sugar, lemon juice and lemon zest. **5.** Put some clean jam jars and lids on a baking tray and then into the oven preheated to 100°C/200°F/Gas 2 for 20 minutes. **6.** Put the pan over a very low heat and, stirring constantly with a wooden spoon, cook until the sugar has completely dissolved and the butter melted. The mixture should not feel gritty when stirred, and there should be no signs of sugar on the back of your spoon. **7.** Now you can begin to cook the curd. Turn the heat up minimally to low and, stirring constantly in a zig-zag pattern, cook the curd until it is thick enough to coat the back of the wooden spoon you are using. This will take about 10 minutes. **8.** Do not stop stirring or leave the pan. And do not let the mixture bubble, which means it is about to boil. If this happens, take the pan from the heat at once and tip the curd into a clean bowl. You may be able to save it by cooling it quickly and then sieving out any scrambled bits. **9.** When the curd is as thick as you want it, or as thick as you dare make it – remembering it will thicken more as it cools – take the pan from the heat. Take the baking tray of jars from the oven. **10.** Pot the curd into the hot jars, using a jam funnel and metal spoon, or a ladle. Cover with the lids and leave to cool. **11.** When the jars are cold, label them and check the lids are firmly screwed on. Store in the fridge.

Passionfruit Curd

It's hard to describe the flavour of passionfruit: it's lush, fragrant, with a touch of acid, and is quite unlike any other taste. Making a rich curd with the strange-looking pulp is the perfect way to capture its elusive beauty. You'll need quite a few fruit, as they yield very little pulp once the crunchy black seeds have been sieved out.

The fruits themselves look unpromising, round or oval, somewhat wrinkled, and very light in weight. Opinion has it that you should buy it very ripe and wrinkled, which is when the perfumed pulp is at its most vivid. I find, however, there is a danger that fruit this ripe will be empty and pretty useless. I chose large, round, unwrinkled fruit for this curd and it worked perfectly. When you cut the fruit open, you will see an unpromising-looking greenish-yellow slime with lots of black seeds, but it will be the perfume that tells you at once that this is something special.

I love to spoon this curd on to scones warm from the oven, spread on crusty bread or, best of all, drizzled over cream-topped meringues.

Yield **approx. 650g** | *Keeps* **4–6 weeks in the fridge**

275g passionfruit (12–14 large fruit), which should
   yield 150ml sieved purée
300g fresh eggs
150g salted butter
225g caster sugar
juice of 1 large lemon, approx. 60ml

1 . Cut the passionfruit in half and scrape the seeds and pulp out into a bowl. Discard the shells.
2 . Rub the pulp through a sieve and discard all but 1 tablespoon of the seeds. Keep these aside.
3 . Whisk the weighed eggs lightly until smooth, and sieve them into your pan. **4 .** Chop the butter into 1cm cubes and put into the pan. Add the sugar, lemon juice and the sieved passionfruit pulp. **5 .** Put some clean jam jars and lids on a baking tray and then into the oven preheated to 100°C/200°F/Gas 2 for 20 minutes. **6 .** Put the pan over a very low heat and, stirring constantly with a wooden spoon, cook until the sugar has completely dissolved and the butter melted. The mixture should not feel gritty when stirred, and there should be no signs of sugar on the back of your spoon. **7 .** Now you can begin to cook the curd. Turn the heat up minimally to low and, stirring constantly in a zig-zag pattern, cook the curd until it is thick enough to coat the back of the wooden spoon. This will take about 10 minutes. **8 .** Do not stop stirring or leave the pan. And do not let the mixture bubble, which means it is about to boil. If this happens, take the pan from the heat at once and tip the curd into a clean bowl. You may be able to save it by cooling it quickly and then sieving out any scrambled bits. **9 .** When the curd is as thick as you want it, or as thick as you dare make it – remembering it will thicken more as it cools – take the pan from the heat. Take the baking tray of jars from the oven. **1 0 .** Stir in the reserved passionfruit seeds. **1 1 .** Pot the curd into the hot jars, using a jam funnel and metal spoon, or a ladle. Cover with the lids and leave to cool. **1 2 .** When the jars are cold, label them and check the lids are firmly screwed on. Store in the fridge.

Rhubarb & Custard Curd

This could more exactly be called rhubarb and vanilla curd, but the taste is exactly that of a bowl of rhubarb and rich custard. Rich and delicious, I serve it on sourdough toast for breakfast or spooned over vanilla *friands* – little almond and egg-white cakes that are very much in vogue at the moment – for an elegant dinner-party dessert. It is also my favourite filling for a home-made Swiss roll or meringue roulade.

Use young or pink forced 'champagne' rhubarb to give the best colour and flavour. Early champagne rhubarb comes into our shops in early January just when we need a flavour fillip.

I use the seeds scraped from a halved vanilla pod, but always put the pod into a jar of caster sugar to impart a rich vanilla flavour.

Yield approx. 750g | *Keeps* 3–4 weeks in the fridge

500g champagne rhubarb
250g fresh eggs
150g salted butter
250g caster sugar
½ vanilla pod

1 . Begin by preparing the rhubarb. Cut the ends from the stems and then slice the stems into 5cm pieces. Put these in a colander and wash well.
2 . Tip the rhubarb into a saucepan along with any water that clings to the stems. Cover the pan and cook over a low heat until the rhubarb breaks down and stews. This will take about 10 minutes.
3 . Tip the contents of the pan into a sieve over the pan in which you will cook the curd. Allow it to drip for 5–10 minutes, then discard the fruit pulp.

4 . Whisk the weighed eggs lightly until smooth, and sieve them into the pan with the rhubarb juice.
5 . Chop the butter into 1cm cubes and put into the pan. Add the sugar. **6 .** With a sharp knife slit open the vanilla pod and scrape out all the seeds into the pan. **7 .** Put some clean jam jars and lids on a baking tray and then into the oven preheated to 100°C/200°F/Gas 2 for 20 minutes. **8 .** Put the pan over a very low heat and, stirring constantly with a wooden spoon, cook until the sugar has completely dissolved and the butter melted. The mixture should not feel gritty when stirred, and there should be no signs of sugar on the back of your spoon. **9 .** Now you can begin to cook the curd. Turn the heat up minimally to low and, stirring constantly in a zig-zag pattern, cook the curd until it is thick enough to coat the back of the wooden spoon. This will take about 10 minutes.
10 . Do not stop stirring or leave the pan. And do not let the mixture bubble, which means it is about to boil. If this happens, take the pan from the heat at once and tip the curd into a clean bowl. You may be able to save it by cooling it quickly and then sieving out any scrambled bits. **11 .** When the curd is as thick as you want it, or as thick as you dare make it – remembering it will thicken more as it cools – take the pan from the heat. Take the baking tray of jars from the oven. **12 .** Pot the curd into the hot jars, using a jam funnel and metal spoon, or a ladle. Cover with the lids and leave to cool. **13 .** When the jars are cold, label them and check the lids are firmly screwed on. Store in the fridge.

Redcurrant Curd

Redcurrants make a delicious summer curd. This recipe uses a slightly different technique than the others: you simply combine all the ingredients – the lightly cooked currant purée, sugar, eggs and butter – in a food processor and whizz until well combined. This rather unprepossessing mixture is then tipped into your pan and you can continue cooking in the usual way.

Wash the currants to get rid of any dust, but there is no need to de-stem them, as the stems will be sieved out when you make the purée. If, by chance, you have any redcurrants in the freezer, they will work well here.

Again I prefer to use salted butter, finding the flavour deeper and more rounded, but feel free to use unsalted if you want a creamier flavour.

Yield **approx. 600g** | *Keeps* **3–4 weeks in the fridge**

500g redcurrants
250g caster sugar
125g salted butter, roughly chopped
275g fresh eggs

1 . Wash the currants under running water to remove any grit or dust. **2 .** Place them in a pan over a low heat with just the water that clings to them, cover the pan, then cook until the fruit softens and boils. This should take about 10 minutes. **3 .** Rub the mixture through a sieve into a bowl. Now place this warm purée, along with the sugar, butter and eggs, in a food processor and whizz until well mixed. **4 .** Tip this mixture into your chosen pan; I use a wide, heavy-bottomed deep sauté pan. **5 .** Put some clean jam jars and lids on a baking tray and then into the oven preheated to 100°C/200°F/Gas 2 for 20 minutes. **6 .** Put the pan over a very low heat and, stirring constantly with a wooden spoon, cook until the sugar has completely dissolved and the butter melted. The mixture should not feel gritty when stirred, and there should be no signs of sugar on the back of your spoon. **7 .** Now you can begin to cook the curd. Turn the heat up minimally to low and, stirring constantly in a zig-zag pattern, cook the curd until it is thick enough to coat the back of the wooden spoon. This will take about 10 minutes. **8 .** Do not stop stirring or leave the pan. And do not let the mixture bubble, which means it is about to boil. If this happens, take the pan from the heat at once and tip the curd into a clean bowl. You may be able to save it by cooling it quickly and then sieving out any scrambled bits. **9 .** When the curd is as thick as you want it, or as thick as you dare make it – remembering it will thicken more as it cools – take the pan from the heat. Take the baking tray of jars from the oven. **10 .** Pot the curd into the hot jars, using a jam funnel and metal spoon, or a ladle. Cover with the lids and leave to cool. **11 .** When the jars are cold, label them and check the lids are firmly screwed on. Store in the fridge.

Lime Curd

This rich tangy curd is made using double cream in place of butter. Using cream means that when eaten cold, straight from the fridge, there is none of the grainy texture you can find when eating a butter-based curd. The principles are the same as when using butter: you cook slowly over a very low heat, stirring constantly, until the curd thickens, then when cold you store the jars in the fridge.

Lovely on toast, better on scones and best of all on hot crumpets, serve this curd for breakfast or at tea-time, and you could use it to make the filling for a wonderful lime meringue pie.

Chose fresh bright green limes, not those shrivelled ones at the bottom of the fruit bowl! You need both very fresh zest and as much juice as possible. I use a Microplane grater to remove every last piece of zest, leaving all the bitter white pith behind, and a lime squeezer, available from good cook shops, to get every last drop of juice out.

Yield **approx. 675g** | *Keeps* **3–4 weeks in the fridge**

4 large or 5 smaller fresh bright green limes
225g fresh eggs
200ml fresh double cream
200g caster sugar

1 . Begin by preparing the limes: scrub the fruit with a scourer under running hot water to remove any wax and dirt. Dry the fruit. **2 .** Using a fine grater, grate the zest from the limes into a heavy, flat-bottomed shallow pan, then halve the fruit and squeeze in the juice, being careful to remove any pips. **3 .** Whisk the weighed eggs lightly until smooth, and sieve them into the pan with the lime juice. **4 .** Stir the cream and sugar into the pan as well. **5 .** Put some clean jam jars and lids on a baking tray and then into the oven preheated to 100°C/200°F/Gas 2 for 20 minutes. **6 .** Put the pan over a very low heat and, stirring constantly with a wooden spoon, cook until the sugar has completely dissolved. The mixture should not feel gritty when stirred, and there should be no signs of sugar on the back of your spoon. **7 .** Now you can begin to cook the curd. Turn the heat up minimally to low and, stirring constantly in a zig-zag pattern, cook the curd until it is thick enough to coat the back of the wooden spoon. This will take about 10 minutes. **8 .** Do not stop stirring or leave the pan. And do not let the mixture bubble, which means it is about to boil. If this happens, take the pan from the heat at once and tip the curd into a clean bowl. You may be able to save it by cooling it quickly and then sieving out any scrambled bits. **9 .** When the curd is as thick as you want it, or as thick as you dare make it – remembering it will thicken more as it cools – take the pan from the heat. Take the baking tray of jars from the oven. **1 0 .** Pot the curd into the hot jars, using a jam funnel and metal spoon, or a ladle. Cover with the lids and leave to cool. **1 1 .** When the jars are cold, label them and check the lids are firmly screwed on. Store in the fridge.

Cranberry Curd

Rich and deep pink, this curd is perfect for breakfast on Christmas morning but don't eat it only then. I find any slice of toast or croissant is enlivened by this lush, cranberry preserve.

I'm using cream here in place of the more usual butter, and for once I'm leaving all the skins and seeds of the fruit in the mix. For a smoother texture these can be sieved out before you cook the curd; the choice is yours.

Fresh or frozen berries will work well here, and you could throw in some orange juice in place of the water, and add some ground cinnamon or a pinch of clove to really ramp up the Christmas flavours.

Yield **approx. 800g** | *Keeps* **3–4 weeks in the fridge**

300g cranberries
100ml water
225g fresh eggs
225g caster sugar
200ml fresh double cream

1 . Wash the cranberries under running water to remove any grit or dust. **2 .** Place them in a pan over a low heat with the water, cover the pan, then cook until the fruit softens and boils. This will take about 10 minutes. Now allow the berries to cool for 5 minutes. **3 .** Put all the ingredients – the berry purée, eggs, sugar and cream – into a food processor and whizz until smooth. Pour the contents of the goblet into your chosen pan. **4 .** Put some clean jam jars and lids on a baking tray and then into the oven preheated to 100°C/200°F/Gas 2 for 20 minutes. **5 .** Put the pan over a very low heat and, stirring constantly with a wooden spoon, cook until the sugar has completely dissolved. The mixture should not feel gritty when stirred, and there should be no signs of sugar on the back of your spoon. **6 .** Now you can begin to cook the curd. Turn the heat up minimally to low and, stirring constantly in a zig-zag pattern, cook the curd until it is thick enough to coat the back of the wooden spoon. This will take about 10 minutes. **7 .** Do not stop stirring or leave the pan. And do not let the mixture bubble, which means it is about to boil. If this happens, take the pan from the heat at once and tip the curd into a clean bowl. You may be able to save it by cooling it quickly and then sieving out any scrambled bits. **8 .** When the curd is as thick as you want it, or as thick as you dare make it – remembering it will thicken more as it cools – take the pan from the heat. Take the baking tray of jars from the oven. **9 .** Pot the curd into the hot jars, using a jam funnel and metal spoon, or a ladle. Cover with the lids and leave to cool. **1 0 .** When the jars are cold, label them and check the lids are firmly screwed on. Store in the fridge.

Gooseberry & Elderflower Curd

Gooseberries and elderflower make a stunning flavour combination, one where both ingredients are made better by the relationship – like good friends who complement each other.

Elderflowers appear in the hedgerows late in May and the first gooseberries are ready for picking in June, so the combination is very much the flavour of an early summer's day.

There are several reasons why I like this recipe, the main one being there is no need to top or tail the gooseberries. You simply wash them to remove any dust and dirt, then poach them in the water that clings to them. Rubbing them through a sieve will remove skins and other fibres.

You can use either a cordial you make yourself or a commercially made one, and frozen gooseberries work perfectly too.

Yield approx. 800g | *Keeps* 3–4 weeks in the fridge

500g gooseberries

225g fresh eggs
125g salted butter

100ml elderflower cordial
200g white caster sugar

1 . Wash the gooseberries under running water to remove any grit or dust. **2 .** Place them in a pan over a low heat with just the water that clings to them, cover the pan, then cook until the fruit softens and boils. This will take about 10 minutes. **3 .** Rub the mixture through a sieve into your chosen heavy-bottomed pan. **4 .** Whisk the weighed eggs lightly until smooth, and sieve these into the pan as well. **5 .** Cut the butter into 1cm cubes, and add these to the pan, along with the elderflower cordial and sugar. **6 .** Put some clean jam jars and lids on a baking tray and then into the oven preheated to 100°C/200°F/Gas 2 for 20 minutes. **7 .** Put the pan over a very low heat and, stirring constantly with a wooden spoon, cook until the sugar has completely dissolved and the butter melted. The mixture should not feel gritty when stirred, and there should be no signs of sugar on the back of your spoon. **8 .** Now you can begin to cook the curd. Turn the heat up minimally to low and, stirring constantly in a zig-zag pattern, cook the curd until it is thick enough to coat the back of the wooden spoon. This will take about 10 minutes. **9 .** Do not stop stirring or leave the pan. And do not let the mixture bubble, which means it is about to boil. If this happens, take the pan from the heat at once and tip the curd into a clean bowl. You may be able to save it by cooling it quickly and then sieving out any scrambled bits. **10 .** When the curd is as thick as you want it, or as thick as you dare make it – remembering it will thicken more as it cools – take the pan from the heat. Take the baking tray of jars from the oven. **11 .** Pot the curd into the hot jars, using a jam funnel and metal spoon, or a ladle. Cover with the lids and leave to cool. **12 .** When the jars are cold, label them and check the lids are firmly screwed on. Store in the fridge.

Blood Orange Curd

I find it's best to use a sharp-tasting fruit for curds: citrus are ideal, but rhubarb, redcurrants and raspberries are excellent too. Here I'm using Sicilian blood oranges, those lovely fruits that arrive in the shops in early January and get their name from their crimson flesh. They make wonderful breakfast juice, and add a lovely blush when used in champagne cocktails. The juice also gives a delicate pink colour to this buttery curd.

Chose fresh firm oranges and don't worry if the skin show no signs of the blush: the flesh inside will often be bright red.

Yield **approx. 650g** | *Keeps* **3–4 weeks in the fridge**

4–5 large blood oranges, to yield 200ml juice
225g fresh eggs
150g salted butter
150g caster sugar

1 . Begin by preparing the fruit: scrub the oranges well using a scourer and hot water to get rid any wax and dirt. **2 .** Finely grate the zest into a heavy-bottomed shallow pan. Halve the oranges and squeeze the juice into the pan, being careful to remove any pips. **3 .** Whisk the weighed eggs lightly until smooth, and sieve into your pan with the orange juice. **4 .** Cut the butter into 1cm cubes, and add to the pan with the sugar. **5 .** Put some clean jam jars and lids on a baking tray and then into the oven preheated to 100°C/200°F/Gas 2 for 20 minutes. **6 .** Put the pan over a very low heat and, stirring constantly with a wooden spoon, cook until the sugar has completely dissolved and the butter melted. The mixture should not feel gritty when stirred, and there should be no signs of sugar on the back of your spoon. **7 .** Now you can begin to cook the curd. Turn the heat up minimally to low and, stirring constantly in a zig-zag pattern, cook the curd until it is thick enough to coat the back of the wooden spoon. This will take about 10 minutes. **8 .** Do not stop stirring or leave the pan. And do not let the mixture bubble, which means it is about to boil. If this happens, take the pan from the heat at once and tip the curd into a clean bowl. You may be able to save it by cooling it quickly and then sieving out any scrambled bits. **9 .** When the curd is as thick as you want it, or as thick as you dare make it – remembering it will thicken more as it cools – take the pan from the heat. Take the baking tray of jars from the oven. **10 .** Pot the curd into the hot jars, using a jam funnel or a ladle. Cover with the lids and leave to cool. **11 .** When the jars are cold, label them and check the lids are firmly screwed on. Store in the fridge.

MARMALADES & CONSERVES

Perfect Marmalades & Conserves

This chapter covers two lovely preserves most often served at breakfast. Here I'm using the term marmalades to describe those made with citrus fruit rather than onions and other assorted vegetables. Conserves tend to have a softer set than jam, and so are blissful when spooned over yoghurt, porridge or a stack of buttermilk pancakes.

Marmalades

Retailers say that we British are turning our backs on marmalade, preferring continental breads such as croissants for the few breakfasts we eat. They predict the total demise of marmalade in the near future. I'm not so sure. I love marmalade, and whilst I don't eat it often at breakfast, I love its bitter tang on buttered crumpets at tea-time and use it to top both steamed sponge puddings and baked ham. There are many stories about how marmalade came into being. My favourite is that a thrifty Scottish housewife, on seeing a load of bitter Seville oranges rotting in a warehouse, decided to preserve them with sugar, and hence Scotland can lay claim to the invention of marmalade. Whilst this is an enticing story, recipes for a precursor to marmalade exist in English cookbooks dating back to the mid 17th century, with some references to bitter orange pastes common in 15th-century literature.

What no one questions is that traditionally marmalade is made with bitter oranges. There is logic in this: Seville oranges are both acidic and high in pectin, so they need only the addition of sugar to make the preserve both set well and be palatable to eat.

Sweet oranges, lemons, limes, grapefruit, clementines and kumquats can all be made into marmalade, but each will need slightly different handling: the sweeter the fruit, the more necessary it is to add lemon juice or citric acid; the more resilient the peel – as in the case of lemons – the more pre-cooking is necessary.

You can vary the flavours of your marmalades by mixing fruits together: adding lemons to oranges, or mixing pink, red and yellow grapefruit. The important point to remember is that the peel must be cooked until it is very soft before the sugar is added.

The type of sugar you use will give different flavours and colours to the finished marmalades. The deep colour of vintage marmalade comes from the use of dark, unrefined sugar and this rich, bitter preserve may be the one most like the first marmalades made in the mid 1600s.

Adding a splash of alcohol to the preserve doesn't improve its keeping qualities but does give a more complex flavor. Whiskey, with its Scottish heritage would seem ideal, but I quite like to add a dash of dark rum to a rich marmalade. Be aware that as the spirit is added at the end of cooking the alcohol will not boil off so there will still be alcohol left in the preserve.

A FEW THINGS TO KNOW ABOUT MAKING MARMALADES

★ There are two stages to making marmalade. In the first stage the fruit is cooked in water until the peel is soft enough to be cut with a wooden spoon. In the second stage the now tender and cut peel is boiled with the sugar and any other ingredients until setting point is reached. Years of trial and error have convinced me that the pre-cooking stage is necessary, as the peel of citrus fruit becomes hard if the sugar is added before the peel has been thoroughly cooked. Once this happens there is no going back, you will have very chewy marmalade.

★ Sometimes the prepared peel is soaked overnight in the required quantity of water to shorten the cooking time. And if you have a pressure cooker, this is the moment to use it. I find in general the peel of fruit cooked at full pressure for 10 minutes, with the pressure allowed to come down slowly, will be ready to continue with the recipe.

★ The fruit can be cooked whole or prepared before cooking. Cooking the fruit whole has several advantages, the most important one being that the peel is much easier to cut finely when it is soft. The liquid in which the whole fruit has been boiled will be rich in pectin and therefore the time taken for stage two will be considerably shorter.

★ If you prepare the peel by cutting it before cooking, the jelly in which the peel is suspended will be clearer, and the peel a crisper cut. This makes for a more attractive marmalade.

★ I have used many different types of sugar when making marmalade and have found that white granulated sugar works just as well as the much more costly preserving sugar. Jam sugar, one that contains pectin, is not usually used for marmalades unless stated in the recipe.

★ For dense, full-flavoured marmalades such as my Old-fashioned Orange and Ginger Marmalade, I use raw, unrefined cane sugar. You can use unbleached granulated sugar in my recipes but the colour will darken as a result.

★ When you add the sugar to the marmalade it is very important that you keep the pan over a low heat to make sure the sugar has dissolved fully before you bring the mixture up to a full rolling boil. This is because undissolved sugar may cause the marmalade to crystallise and have an unpleasant texture. Timings involved in dissolving sugar will vary, according to sugar type, heat of liquid etc. but you can easily tell if the sugar has not dissolved: when you stir the marmalade the sugar will feel gritty against the sides of the pan and if you look at the back of the wooden spoon you are using you will see tiny grains of undissolved sugar.

★ You will need a large heavy-bottomed pan. This does not have to be a dedicated preserving pan but it must be a pan that is non-reactive or acid-resistant. I use a giant enamelled iron casserole dish, but stainless steel is good also. Choose a pan that is wider than it is tall. A good surface area is necessary to allow for rapid evaporation of water when boiling for a set.

★ Use only fresh good-quality fruit. You only want to preserve the best, for citrus has a predilection for picking up mould, especially unwaxed fruit. I throw all mouldy fruit away, as the taint can seep into the seemingly fresh parts.

★ The skin of citrus fruit is porous so it is often given a thin wax coating to extend its shelf life. Therefore it's necessary to wash your fruit well in hot water, scrubbing it with a vegetable brush or scourer to remove this wax. Even if the fruit is not waxed it will need a good wash to remove any dirt or mould spores.

★ It is perfectly fine to re-use old jam jars and lids for marmalade, but with this proviso: the jars must be spotlessly clean and not chipped or damaged. Any lids must be spotless too, with no sign of damage or rust.

★ As citrus fruit is usually high in pectin, marmalade, especially when made with Seville oranges, sets quite easily. The exact time you will need to cook it will depend on how large your pan is, but the recipes will give you a guide.

★ Getting ready to test for a set is important but quite easy. As the mixture boils for the second time it will reduce and eventually reach setting point. You can tell when this point nears, as the mixture will boil more sluggishly, and the bubbles will 'plop' rather than froth. I have given times when you should begin testing for a set, but don't worry if you find the time it takes to cook your marmalade exceeds these.

★ It may be necessary to skim off any scum that rises to the surface as the mixture boils. To do this you will need a slotted spoon, or skimming spoon, and a small bowl of hot water. Use the spoon to skim some scum off, then rinse in hot water and skim again.

★ When testing for a set, you will have a couple of small china or glass plates or saucers ready in the freezer. When you want to do the first test turn off the heat under the pan and spoon a little marmalade on to one of these plates. Leave this until it has cooled, about 30 seconds to a minute, then push the side of the mixture with your finger. If you can see a wrinkle, the mixture is ready. If the marmalade is still liquid you will need to boil for a few more minutes then test again. I test at 2-minute intervals. It is very important to remove the pan from the heat while you test.

★ As you near setting point, stir the mixture often as the peel has a tendency to fall to the bottom and stick where it will soon burn. A good stir with a wooden spoon prevents this.

★ Once the marmalade has reached setting point, let it sit for 5 minutes, then stir it gently to help distribute the peel evenly in the jelly.

★ If you are adding some whiskey, brandy or rum to your marmalade now is the time to do it. Stir about 50–75 ml of spirit into your batch of marmalade once it has reached setting point.

★ Always pot the hot marmalade into hot jars. I keep mine, along with the lids, on a baking tray in the oven preheated to 100ºC/200ºF/Gas 2 until I need them, but for at least 15 minutes.

★ I keep the jars on the baking tray to fill, and use a jam funnel. The funnel is not essential, a small ladle or a jug will do, but you really want to try and avoid getting the jars too messy.
20 As soon as you have potted the marmalade, cover the jars with the lids. I use metal ones but you can use waxed paper and cellophane.

★ Once the jars have cooled, check the lids are screwed on tightly, and label the jars. You may think you'll remember what is in which, but take it from me you won't.

★ I always add the date to my labels and a list of any additional ingredients such as brandy so I can avoid giving jars of, say, spicy ginger marmalade to the wrong people.

★ Like other preserves, marmalades should be stored in a cool, dark cupboard or, if you have one, a pantry.

★ Marmalades keep well but even those made with white granulated sugar will darken a little with age. This change in colour is nothing to worry about and indeed marmalade that is several years old takes on a wonderful rich ripe flavor, maturing a little like a chutney.

★ Marmalade is a wonderful ingredient to use in all sorts of recipes so don't worry if you find yourself with rather more jars than you think you can eat. I use marmalade mixed with mustard powder to glaze hams and pork roasts. I stir a spoonful or two into pork casseroles and lamb tagines.

★ I mix marmalade, fresh orange juice and a shot of Cointreau into thickly whipped cream and use to fill sponge cakes, profiteroles and meringues. And marmalade makes a wonderful topping to a steamed sponge pudding.

How to Make the Perfect Jar of Marmalade

Home-made marmalade is a treat in so many ways. The best oranges for making it – bitter Seville oranges from Spain – come into our shops after Christmas in those bleak months of January and February. They are truly seasonal and so you must buy them when you see them, as they vanish quickly. If I don't have time to make the marmalade at once, I simply freeze the oranges until I do.
So marmalade brings colour into our kitchen and the most wonderful aromas of sugar and citrus. Filled jars sit like lanterns on the side, lighting the dark drear days.

I make many different sorts of marmalade, but this one is the first I tried, and I still make it every year. The recipe comes from a friend's mother and is excellent for beginners. She always minced the fruit using an old-fashioned mincer, but I chop it using a sharp knife on a board.

When you cut the peel do take the time to cut it finely: as the marmalade cooks with the sugar, the peel absorbs the syrup and swells to about double the size.

Yield approx. 1.6–2kg | *Keeps* 1 year

Ingredients

7 Seville oranges
2 sweet oranges
1 large lemon
1.8 litres water
1.4kg white granulated sugar

Equipment

Scales and a measuring jug ★ Vegetable brush or scourer ★ Large heavy-bottomed, non-reactive preserving pan with a lid ★ Slotted spoon and small bowl of hot water ★ 2 large clean glass or china bowls ★ Some glass jars with lids, washed and dried ★ Baking tray ★ 2–3 small china or glass plates or saucers ★ Sharp knife ★ Metal tablespoon ★ Chopping board (or a mincer or food processor) ★ Sieve ★ Small square of muslin and a piece of string ★ Wooden spoon ★ 1 metal teaspoon ★ Jam funnel or ladle

1 . Begin by washing the fruit well in hot water and scrubbing it with a small vegetable brush. Seville oranges are seldom waxed but the other fruit might be. **2 .** Place the washed fruit in the preserving pan, adding the water. Bring this to the boil, cover the pan with a lid, and simmer until the fruit is very soft. This will take about 50–60 minutes. **3 .** Take the pan from the heat, lift out the fruit using a slotted spoon, and place in a bowl. Leave it until it's cool enough to touch. **4 .** When the fruit is cool enough to touch, halve the oranges and lemons, cutting them over the bowl to catch any juice that comes out. As you cut each piece of fruit in half, squeeze it gently and with the tablespoon scoop the pips and membranes out into the bowl. **5 .** Place the empty fruit shells on a chopping board and slice them finely by hand. Alternatively you can mince the peel, or whizz briefly in a food processor. **6 .** Now you need to measure the liquid you cooked the fruit in. Pour the cooking liquid into a measuring jug: you may need to empty this into the second clean bowl if

your jug is a small one. Now strain in the liquid that has gathered in the bowl the fruit cooled in. Add up the quantities. You need 1.5 litres of liquid; if you have less than this, make it up with water. **7 .** Now collect together any solids left in the sieve, and the contents of the pips, pith and membrane bowl. Wrap these in a small square of muslin, tying tightly with a piece of string. **8 .** Wash the preserving pan and put in the prepared peel. Add the bag of pips and the cooking liquid. **9 .** Put some clean jam jars and lids on a baking tray and then into the oven preheated to 100°C/200°F/Gas 2 for 20 minutes. Place two to three small plates or saucers in the freezer to chill. **10 .** Place the pan on the hob and stir in the sugar. Cook over a low heat, stirring with a wooden spoon, until the sugar has completely dissolved, and there is no trace of grittiness in the pan or on the back of the spoon. **11 .** Once the sugar has dissolved, turn up the heat and bring the mixture to the boil. Cook the marmalade at a full rolling boil, one that can't be

stirred down with the spoon, for 10 minutes. The marmalade will reduce and thicken. **12 .** Now test for a set. Turn off the heat and take one of the plates from the freezer. Spoon a small amount of marmalade on to the plate. If, after the marmalade has cooled slightly, the surface wrinkles when the side is pushed gently with your finger, you are ready to pot. **13 .** If the marmalade is still runny, return the pan to the heat and boil for a further 2 minutes, then switch off and test again. **14 .** Once the marmalade has reached setting point, turn off the heat, discard the muslin bag and leave it to stand for 5 minutes before stirring to redistribute the peel. Take the baking tray of jars from the oven at the same time. **15 .** Pot the marmalade into the hot jars. I use a jam funnel to help with this but a ladle will do. Put the lids on loosely and leave to cool. **16 .** When the jars are cold, label them, and check the lids are firmly screwed on. Store in a cool, dark place.

Old-fashioned Orange & Ginger Marmalade

This is a dark, full-flavoured chunky marmalade, rather an old-fashioned taste, the sort you might see in rather proper hotel breakfast rooms. I think it's time to drag it into the light, as the flavour is amazing, ginger perfectly complementing the tangy Seville oranges.

I use two different types of ginger to layer the flavour: fresh ginger cooked with the oranges gives heat to the mix, then stem ginger added to the second stage gives wonderful pings of soft spicy ginger when you eat it.

You can choose how dark you want this preserve to be by changing the type of sugar you use. Light muscovado or unrefined granulated sugar are best, but if you want a really treacly result, use a dark soft raw sugar.

Yield approx. 1.6–2kg | *Keeps* 1 year

1.25kg Seville oranges
2 litres water
110g fresh root ginger
1.5kg unrefined granulated sugar
1 x 350g jar preserved ginger in syrup, finely sliced (keep the syrup too)
75ml whisky (optional)

1. Scrub the oranges in hot water, using a scourer, and put into your deep preserving pan with the water. **2.** Peel the fresh ginger. I find scraping the skin off with the side of a teaspoon the most effective way to do this. Chop into 1cm cubes and put into the pan with the oranges. **3.** Put the pan on the heat, cover with the lid and simmer the fruit until very soft, about 45–60 minutes. You should be able to cut the peel of the oranges with a wooden spoon. **4.** Take the pan from the heat. Using a slotted spoon remove both ginger and oranges from the pan and place them in a bowl to cool slightly. **5.** Once the fruit is cool enough to handle, cut the oranges in half and scrape out all the pips and membranes inside. Wrap these, along with the ginger, in a small square of muslin and tie up with a piece of string. **6.** Place the empty fruit shells on a chopping board and, using a sharp knife, finely slice them. **7.** Measure the cooking liquid and make this up to 1.3 litres by adding water. Put the sugar, peel and bag of membranes in the pan. **8.** Put the clean jam jars and lids on a baking tray and then into the oven preheated to 100°C/200°F/Gas 2 for 20 minutes. Place two to three small plates or saucers in the freezer to chill. **9.** Put the pan over a low heat, stirring with a wooden spoon until the sugar has fully dissolved, and there is no trace of grittiness in the pan or on the back of the spoon. **10.** Add the finely sliced preserved ginger and the ginger syrup to the pan, then turn up the heat. When the mixture comes to the boil, cook at a full rolling boil, one that can't be stirred down with the spoon, for 10 minutes. **11.** It may be necessary to skim off any scum that rises to the surface as the mixture boils. To do this you will need a slotted spoon and a bowl of hot water. Use the spoon to skim some scum then rinse in the hot water and skim again. **12.** Once the marmalade has been cooking for 10 minutes, test for a set. Turn off the heat and take one of the plates from the freezer. Spoon a small amount of marmalade on to the plate. If, after the marmalade has cooled slightly, the surface wrinkles when the side is pushed gently with your finger, you are ready to pot. **1 3 .** If the marmalade is still runny return the pan to the heat and boil for a further 2 minutes, then switch off and test again. **1 4 .** Once the marmalade has reached setting point turn off the heat, discard the muslin bag, stir in the whisky if you're using it, and leave it to stand for 5 minutes before stirring again. Take the baking tray of jars from the oven at the same time. **1 5 .** Pot the marmalade into the hot jars, using a jam funnel if available, and cover loosely with the lids. Leave to cool. **1 6 .** When the jars are cold, label them, and check the lids are firmly screwed on. Store in a cool, dark place.

Grapefruit Marmalade: Pink, Ruby or Yellow

Pink grapefruit marmalade is a real favourite in our house, its colour and tanginess making it a perfect accompaniment to a couple of slices of well-buttered sourdough toast, but I find any colour of grapefruit makes a good marmalade.

Yield **approx. 1.6–2kg** | *Keeps* **1 year**

4 fresh grapefruit, approx. 1.5kg
1.5 litres water
1.5kg white granulated sugar
juice of 2 large lemons

1 . Scrub the grapefruit well under hot water, using a vegetable brush or scourer, until all wax has been removed. **2 .** Using a sharp knife halve the fruit and squeeze out all the juice. I find the attachment on my food processor helps here, but any citrus juicer will do. Put in a jug and keep in the fridge. **3 .** Make sure you keep the pips, placing them in a separate bowl. **4 .** Using a sharp spoon scrape any membranes and pith from the fruit shells and add these to the pips. Tie the pips, pith and membranes in a small square of muslin and tie up with a piece of string. **5 .** Finely slice the peel, putting it into a deep china or glass bowl. Pour over the water, cover and leave overnight in a cool room or the fridge. **6 .** When you are ready to cook the marmalade, put some clean jam jars and lids on a baking tray and then into the preheated oven at 100°C/200°F/Gas 2 for 20 minutes. Place two to three small plates or saucers in the freezer to chill. **7 .** Put the peel, its soaking water and the bag of pith into a wide heavy-bottomed pan and place this on the heat. Bring the mixture to a simmer, loosely cover with a lid and cook the peel until it is soft enough to cut with a wooden spoon. This should take about 25 minutes. **8 .** Once the peel is cooked, tip in the sugar and both the lemon and the grapefruit juices, then stir over a low heat until the sugar has completely dissolved and there is no trace of grittiness in the pan or on the back of the spoon. **9 .** Bring the marmalade to the boil and cook at a full rolling boil, one that cannot be stirred down, for about 10 minutes. **10 .** Skim off any scum that rises to the surface with a slotted spoon, rinsing it in a bowl of hot water between skims. **11 .** Once the marmalade has been cooking for 10 minutes, test for a set. Turn off the heat and take one of the plates from the freezer. Spoon a small amount of marmalade on to a plate. If, after the marmalade has cooled slightly, the surface wrinkles when the side is pushed gently with your finger, you are ready to pot. **12 .** If the marmalade is still runny return the pan to the heat and boil for a further 2 minutes then switch off and test again. **13 .** Once the marmalade has reached setting point turn off the heat, discard the muslin bag, and leave it to stand for 5 minutes before stirring again. Take the baking tray of jars from the oven at the same time. **14 .** Pot the marmalade into the hot jars, using a jam funnel if available, and cover loosely with the lids. Leave to cool. **15 .** When the jars are cold, label them, and check the lids are firmly screwed on. Store in a cool, dark place.

Pressure-cooker Lemon Marmalade

Using a pressure cooker for the initial stage of making marmalade cuts down the time it takes to complete the recipe. The peel softens quickly under pressure, but I find the best way to finish the cooking is in a wide, open preserving pan. If you are not using a pressure cooker, cook the lemons in 1.5 litres of water in a covered pan until the skins are soft enough to cut with a wooden spoon, about 60 minutes. Continue as below using 1 litre of the cooking liquid.

Yield **approx. 1.2–1.4kg** | *Keeps* **1 year**

1kg lemons
1 litre water
1kg white granulated sugar

1 . Begin by scrubbing the lemons well. I wash unwaxed ones in hot water to remove any dust or mould spores, and scrub waxed ones with a vegetable brush or scourer. **2 .** Place the fruit and the water in the pressure cooker. Close the lid and place over a moderate heat to bring up to pressure. **3 .** Cook at high pressure for 10 minutes then allow the pressure to come down slowly. **4 .** Once the lid has been released open it and allow the fruit to cool until you can touch it. Check the peel is very tender; you should be able to cut it with a wooden spoon. **5 .** Take the lemons from the pan and place them in a bowl so that when you cut them in half you will catch the juice. Reserve all the cooking liquid to make the marmalade. **6 .** When the lemons are cool enough to touch, halve them, and carefully scoop out all the pith, pips and membranes, using a metal spoon.

Save these, then wrap them in a small square of muslin and tie up with a piece of string. **7 .** Finely slice the empty lemon shells. Place these slices in a preserving pan along with the cooking liquid. Strain the collected juices from the bowl through a sieve and then place in the pan, along with the muslin bag. **8 .** Put some clean jam jars and lids on a baking tray and then into the oven preheated to 100°C/200°F/Gas 2 for 20 minutes. Place two to three small plates or saucers into the freezer to chill. **9 .** Now add the sugar to the pan, and put over a low heat, stirring with a wooden spoon until the sugar has completely dissolved and there is no trace of grittiness in the pan or on the back of the spoon. **10 .** Bring the mixture up to the boil and cook at a full rolling boil, one that cannot be stirred down, for 10 minutes before you test for a set. **11 .** Turn off the heat and take one of the plates from the freezer. Spoon a small amount of marmalade on to the plate. If, after the marmalade has cooled slightly, the surface wrinkles when the side is pushed gently with your finger, you are ready to pot. **12 .** If the marmalade is still runny return the pan to the heat and boil for a further 2 minutes then switch off and test again. **13 .** Once the marmalade has reached setting point, turn off the heat, discard the muslin bag and leave it to stand for 5 minutes before stirring again. Take the baking tray of jars from the oven at the same time. **14 .** Pot the marmalade into the hot jars and cover loosely with the lids. Leave to cool. **15 .** When the jars are cold, label them, and check the lids are firmly screwed on. Store in a cool, dark place.

Clementine Marmalade

When you are making this marmalade you have a choice as to how you wish the finished preserve to look: you can shred the cooked peel with a sharp knife, which is perfectly possible but a little time-consuming, or you can give the peel a quick, and I do mean quick, whizz in a food processor. The first will give a clearer looking marmalade, the latter a more cloudy one. Either will work well and taste good, so it is a simple matter of aesthetics.

I have added some orange liqueur to my marmalade at the end of cooking. Be aware that this does add a little alcohol to the finished preserve: some bubbles off in the vapour, but it is not completely cooked out. I use whatever orange-flavoured spirit I have in the cupboard, but Curaçao, made with the bitter oranges that grow on this Caribbean island, works beautifully.

Clementines are dessert oranges, so are sweeter than the more usual marmalade oranges, Seville oranges. Whilst they have very thin skins, clementines still need some pre-cooking to give a tender preserve. Mandarin oranges, a cousin of the clementine, can be used successfully in this recipe.

Yield **approx. 1–1.2kg** | *Keeps* **1 year**

750g clementines
100ml fresh lemon juice
500ml water
750g white granulated sugar
50–75ml Curaçao (or other orange liqueur)

1 . Start by washing the fruit in hot water. This will help remove any wax, dust or mould spores from the skin. I scrub mine gently with a vegetable brush. **2 .** Cut each clementine in half and remove and discard any pips. **3 .** If you are slicing by hand, cut the whole fruit into very thin slices and pile these into the preserving pan. If using a food processor, place the halved fruit into the processor bowl and whizz, using the pulse button, for a few seconds until the fruit is roughly chopped. Tip this into your preserving pan. **4 .** Add the lemon juice and water and bring the mixture up to a simmer. Cook at a low boil for about 7 minutes, or until the peel is very soft. **5 .** Put some clean jam jars and lids on a baking tray and into the oven preheated to 100°C/200°F/Gas 2 for 20 minutes. Place two to three small plates or saucers into the freezer to chill. **6 .** Turn off the heat under the preserving pan, and add the sugar. Now place the pan over a low heat and stir the sugar in until it has completely dissolved, and there is no trace of grittiness in the pan or visible on the back of the spoon. **7 .** Turn the heat back on and bring the mixture to the boil. Cook at a full rolling boil for 4 minutes. **8 .** Turn off the heat and test for a set by spooning a small amount on to a cold plate. If, after a few minutes, the surface of the jam wrinkles, you are ready to pot the marmalade. If the marmalade is still runny, boil it for a further 2 minutes then switch off and test again. **9 .** Once you have reached setting point turn off the heat and allow the marmalade to sit for 5 minutes, before stirring in the Curaçao. Take the baking tray of jars from the oven at the same time. **1 0 .** Pot the marmalade into the hot jars, using a jam funnel if available, and cover loosely with the lids. Leave to cool. **1 1 .** When cold, label and check the lids are firmly screwed on. Store in a cool, dark place.

Conserves

Conserves cover a range of preserves that are not necessarily set firm. In Britain we like our jam to be able to mound on the spoon, whereas continental conserves are looser and so can run off toast or bread. There are, however, a great many definitions of what makes a conserve. One lovely one I found states that to conserve is 'to use or manage natural resources wisely, to preserve and save'. I think that resonates with my using the term to mean a softer-set fruit preserve. Often these conserves are made without using pectin; they are simply cooked until thick, then potted, when they will thicken a little more as they cool. They may have a lower sugar content than jams and jellies, which many find attractive. You should be aware, however, that low-sugar preserves do not keep well and need to be stored in the fridge and eaten within two weeks once opened, otherwise they will lose their colour and texture and may go mouldy.

Conserves can be made with dried fruits and nuts too, so are ideal to make when fresh fruits are not around. I make them in relatively small batches and pot them into smallish pots. Having a softer set than jam and a more luscious texture, conserves are perfect spooned over yoghurt or porridge, or used to top waffles and pancakes.

A FEW THINGS TO KNOW ABOUT MAKING CONSERVES

★ With conserves, as with other preserves, choose the best and fullest-flavoured examples of the fruits you are going to use. Make sure there is no bruising and mould on the fruit, then prepare it as the recipe instructs.

★ I use granulated white sugar for conserves, but an unrefined granulated sugar will give another layer of taste. This would work well in the dried apricot conserve recipe on page 106. Whatever sugar you choose it must be fully dissolved in your preserve before the mixture comes to the boil. Timings involved in dissolving sugar will vary, according to sugar type, heat of liquid etc. You must check that the pan no longer feels gritty, and that there are no signs of sugar crystals on your wooden spoon before continuing with the recipe.

★ Conserves can contain nuts, or have nuts as their main ingredient. When choosing nuts it is good to remember that they have a tendency to become rancid if stored at room temperature. I store my nuts in the freezer or buy them fresh, checking the use-by date on the packets.

Whilst it is slightly more effort, shelling and grinding the nuts yourself often gives a better-tasting result.

★ Once again I urge you to use freshly ground spices for conserves, preparing them as you need them, to capture all their wonderful flavour and perfume.

★ Whilst we are not looking for a pectin set with these conserves, there are occasions when you need to add acid to balance the sweetness. I prefer to use natural citrus fruit here rather than citric acid powder. Lemons, limes or sharp oranges all work well.

★ The method of making conserves varies from recipe to recipe, so read each one through before you begin

★ Skimming is not usually necessary, but if your conserve has some scum on the surface, simply skim this off, using a slotted spoon rinsed in a bowl of hot water between skims.

★ It is important to use clean sterilised jars for potting. Wash your chosen jars and their lids in hot soapy water, dry them then sterilise them in an oven preheated to 100ºC/200ºF/Gas 2 for 15–20 minutes.

★ I prefer to use lids to cover all my preserves as I feel they give the best seal. Check your lids, like your jars, are clean and in good condition before proceeding as above.

★ Don't forget to label and date your conserves before storing them in a cool, dark place. Once open, conserves should be stored in the fridge.

How to Make the Perfect Jar of Dried Apricot Conserve

I like to make conserves with fruits I would not make jam from, choosing exciting combinations, and this one made with dried fruit and nuts is a perfect example.

There is no need to worry about pectin here, the preserve is simply simmered until thick. You can use unbleached apricots but I'm afraid I prefer the look of the brighter orange ones. Here I've added pistachio nuts, lime and brandy to ramp up the taste. If you don't like nuts in preserves, simply leave out the pistachios. If I'm going to spoon this on to yoghurt for breakfast I leave out the brandy!

Yield approx. 1.2kg | *Keeps* 6 months

Ingredients

500g ready-to-eat dried apricots

500ml water

2 large limes

450g white granulated sugar

100g shelled unsalted pistachio nuts

75ml brandy

Equipment

Scales and a measuring jug ★ 1 large glass or china bowl ★ Sieve ★ Large heavy-bottomed, non-reactive preserving pan ★ Chopping board and knife ★ Vegetable brush or scourer ★ Microplane or other fine grater ★ Some glass jars with lids, washed and dried ★ Baking tray ★ Wooden spoon ★ Large metal spoon ★ Labels

1. Put the apricots and water into a bowl and leave to soak overnight. **2.** Now drain them through a sieve, pouring the soaking liquid into the preserving pan. Roughly chop the apricots and place in the pan with the water. **3.** Scrub the limes well with a small vegetable brush under hot water, then dry them and grate the zest finely into the pan. Squeeze the juice from the limes through a sieve into the pan. **4.** Put some clean jam jars and their lids on to a baking tray and then into the oven preheated to 100°C/200°F/Gas 2 for 20 minutes. **5.** Put the pan on a gentle heat and bring the mixture to a simmer. Cook for 5 minutes, stirring with a wooden spoon, until the apricots begin to soften. **6.** Now stir in the sugar with the wooden spoon, keeping the pan over a low heat until the sugar has completely dissolved and there is no trace of grittiness in the pan or on the back of the spoon. **7.** Bring the mixture to the boil, then turn the heat down and simmer until thick, about 10 minutes. The conserve should be thick enough to need a gentle nudge to fall from the spoon. It should not be liquid. **8.** Roughly chop the nuts then stir them and the brandy into the conserve. **9.** Take the baking tray of jars from the oven, and leave to rest for 5 minutes. **10.** Spoon the preserve into the hot jars, cover loosely with the lids, and leave to cool. **11.** When the jars are cold, label them, and make sure the lids are firmly screwed on. Store in a cool, dark place.

Chestnut & Vanilla Conserve

This is a truly lovely preserve to make. Yes, it is a bit of a chore peeling the chestnuts, but once done the rest is simplicity. Make it at Christmas and give a couple of jars to friends. They will love it spread on toast, mixed into whipped cream or spooned straight from the jar! Be sure, though, to keep at least one jar for yourself. I add a tablespoon or so of brandy to mine – not strictly necessary, but nice.

Make sure the chestnuts are fresh, as they rot quite quickly, and it is very tedious to find you have to discard half the nuts having peeled them.

Yield **approx. 600g** | *Keeps* **3 months**

500g fresh chestnuts, 350g peeled weight
175g white granulated sugar
175ml water
1 plump vanilla pod
½ tablespoons brandy

1 . Using a sharp knife, make a small slit in each nut, about 1cm long, and pop them into a saucepan. **2 .** Cover the nuts with water, bring them to the boil, then cook at a simmer, uncovered, for 25 minutes. You may need to top up the water if the level falls below the nuts. **3 .** Take the pan from the heat. **4 .** There are two ways of peeling chestnuts, either hot or cold. The skins come off quite easily when the nuts are hot, having just been cooked. Simply drain the nuts, then peel off the skin, making sure you remove all the furry under-skin. If you drain the nuts and leave them to get cold, you can simply cut them in half and scoop the nut meat out of the skins with a small spoon, again avoiding the furry under-skin. Put the nut meat into a blender or food processor. **5 .** Place some small clean jam jars and lids into the oven preheated to 100°C/200°F/Gas 2 for 20 minutes. **6 .** Now mix the sugar and measured water in a clean preserving or other large pan and put this over a low heat, stirring occasionally until the sugar dissolves and there is no trace of grittiness in the pan or visible on the back of the spoon. **7 .** Using a sharp knife split open the vanilla pod and scrape out the seeds. Add these to the nuts and pop the pod into the syrup mixture. **8 .** Once the sugar has dissolved in the water boil the syrup, at a full rolling boil, for 3 minutes. Remove the pan from the heat and take out the pod. **9 .** Now tip the hot syrup on to the nuts, and whizz until smooth. **10 .** Scrape this mixture back into the cleaned pan and cook, stirring constantly, over a moderate heat until the mixture is very thick. **11 .** Take the pan from the heat and stir in the brandy. **12 .** Take the baking tray of jars from the oven, and spoon the conserve into the hot jars, packing it down well. Loosely cover with the lids and leave to cool. **13 .** When the jars are cold, label them, and make sure the lids are firmly screwed on. Store in a cool, dark place.

Melon & Vanilla Conserve

Melon may seem an unusual choice for a preserve, but there is a long history of it being used for 'spoon sweets' in Greece and Turkey. These very liquid and, to my mind, overwhelmingly sweet delicacies are served in tiny spoons with tea or coffee as a welcoming snack. As they are served in spoons they don't need to be very set and so are often made simply with a great deal of sugar and the fruit. I prefer to use less sugar, adding acid and pectin to help the conserve stay on my toast.

Do use ripe, highly scented melons for this recipe. I favour Cantaloupe, or Charentais as it is often called. It is usual to add a second flavour to melon conserves, a common pairing being ginger, but I like the more subtle notes of vanilla, cardamom or saffron.

Yield **approx. 1.2kg** | *Keeps* **1 year**

1kg melon flesh, prepared weight
125ml fresh lemon juice
700g jam sugar
seeds scraped from 1 vanilla pod, or ½ teaspoon
  finely ground cardamom

1 . To prepare the melons peel them, removing all the thick outside rind and then carefully scrape out all the seeds. Keep as much of the inner flesh as you can, it's here the greatest flavour lies. Chop the flesh into 1.5cm cubes. **2 .** Now put the melon into a large glass or non-reactive bowl, and pour over the lemon juice. Add the sugar and, using a large metal spoon, toss everything together gently. Allow this to sit for 24 hours. **3 .** Put some clean jam jars and lids on a baking tray and then into the oven preheated to 100°C/200°F/Gas 2 for 20 minutes. Place two to three small plates or saucers in the freezer to chill. **4 .** Carefully strain all the liquid that has collected in the bowl into a clean preserving or other large pan and bring this to a simmer, stirring to check all the sugar has dissolved and there is no trace of grittiness in the pan or visible on the back of the spoon. **5 .** Once there is no grittiness left, turn up the heat and bring to a boil. Boil rapidly to reduce the liquid by roughly half, about 4–5 minutes. **6 .** Put in the melon cubes and simmer for a further 4–5 minutes to cook the fruit. **7 .** After 5 minutes turn off the heat and test for a set by spooning a small amount on to a cold plate or saucer. If, after the conserve has cooled slightly, the surface wrinkles when pushed gently with your finger, you are ready to pot it. **8 .** If not, re-boil for a further 2 minutes then switch off and test again. The conserve should cook for between 7 and 10 minutes in total. **9 .** Now skim off any scum with a slotted spoon, rinsing it in a bowl of hot water between skims. **10 .** Once this is done stir in the vanilla, cardamom or whatever flavouring you have chosen. **11 .** Allow the conserve to stand for about 5 minutes, and stir again. Take the baking tray of jars from the oven at the same time. **12 .** Spoon the conserve into the hot jars, cover loosely with the lids, and leave to cool. **13 .** Once the jars are cold, label them, and make sure the lids are firmly screwed on. Store in a cool, dark place.

Orange, Cinnamon & Cranberry Conserve

Cranberries are such a delightful arrival in our kitchens in winter. They bring not only their particular sharp fresh taste to food, but also colour in an otherwise sad palette of browns and dark greens. I use cranberries in many ways: yes, with the turkey lunch on Christmas Day, as an added ingredient in stews and chutneys, and in a lovely deep garnet vodka that keeps out the winter chills.

This soft-set conserve, using as it does those other winter favourites, cinnamon and orange, makes a colourful and tasty topping for toast and crusty bread, but it can also be spooned on to yoghurt and is a blissful addition to a plate of steaming porridge.

It is necessary to cook the fruit before adding the sugar as the skins of the cranberries can toughen if the sugar is added too soon. So don't miss this part of the recipe.

If you have a spice mill, grind your cinnamon just before you use it for extra fragrance.

Yield **approx. 1kg** | *Keeps* **4 months**

4 medium sweet oranges

1 lemon

500g fresh cranberries

350g white granulated sugar

1 teaspoon ground cinnamon, or 4cm cinnamon
  stick, freshly ground

1 . Begin by preparing the fruit. Scrub the oranges and lemon under hot water, using a vegetable brush or scourer. Wash the cranberries under cold running water, and leave to drain. **2 .** Grate the zest of two of the oranges and the lemon into a large preserving pan. Squeeze the juice from the lemon, and keep this separately. **3 .** Using a sharp knife, cut all the peel from all the oranges and discard this. Now cut the flesh into chunks, and place these in the pan. **4 .** Add the cranberries and place on a low heat. Cover the pan with the lid, and cook at a gentle simmer for 10–15 minutes, stirring occasionally, until the cranberries soften and start to pop. **5 .** Now tip in the sugar, lemon juice and cinnamon, and stir until the sugar has fully dissolved and there is no trace of grittiness in the pan or visible on the back of the spoon. **6 .** Meanwhile, place some jam jars and lids on a baking tray and into the oven preheated to 100°C/200°F/Gas 2 for 20 minutes. When ready to pot, remove the tray and leave to rest for 5 minutes. **7 .** Turn up the heat under the pan, and simmer until the mixture is thick, about 10 minutes. There is no testing for a set here. **8 .** Once the conserve is thick, spoon into the hot jars, cover loosely with the lids, and leave to cool. **9 .** Once the jars are cold, label them, and make sure the lids are firmly screwed on. Store in a cool, dark place.

Persimmon, Lime & Ginger Conserve

This is a great preserve to make in those bleak winter months when autumn fruit has finished and before the marmalade oranges arrive.

Originally from the Far East, persimmons are widely grown in southern Europe, Israel and the Americas. The high tannin content of the fruit makes it totally unpalatable when under-ripe, but once ripened the fruit is amazingly sweet and tender.

It is cooked in much the same way as a marmalade. Test for a set at the times given and make sure you do not over-cook the persimmons as they become tough.

Yield **approx. 800g** | *Keeps* **6 months**

4 medium sweet oranges
700g, about 4–5 large, very ripe, Hachiya persimmons
500g jam sugar
3 large limes
20g fresh root ginger, peeled weight

1 . Begin by carefully peeling the fruit. When the persimmons are very ripe this is simple and the skin just peels off. A potato peeler can be used if necessary. **2 .** Roughly chop the fruit into largeish pieces and place in a large bowl. Add the sugar and stir in. **3 .** Scrub the limes well, using a scourer. Using a Microplane or similar grater, finely grate the zest from two of the limes into the bowl then add the juice of all three. Using the same grater, grate in the ginger. **4 .** Leave the mixture for 2–3 hours, stirring occasionally, to allow the sugar to begin to dissolve.

5 . Meanwhile put some clean jam jars and lids on a baking tray and then into the oven preheated to 100°C/200°F/Gas 2 for 20 minutes. Place two to three small plates or saucers in the freezer to chill. **6 .** Once the sugar has begun to dissolve, tip the contents of the bowl into a wide heavy-bottomed pan and place over a low heat, stirring occasionally, until the sugar has dissolved and there is no trace of grittiness in the pan or on the back of the spoon. Bring the mixture up to a full rolling boil and cook for 4 minutes. **7 .** Turn off the heat and test for a set by placing a small spoonful of conserve on one of the cold plates and leaving for a few moments. Gently press the side of the conserve, and if the surface wrinkles, the conserve is ready. **8 .** If not, bring back to the boil and cook for another minute, re-testing as above. **9 .** Once you've reached setting point, remove from the heat, and let the conserve rest for 5 minutes. Take the baking tray of jars from the oven at the same time. **10 .** Spoon the conserve into the hot jars, loosely cover with the lids, and leave to cool. **11 .** When the jars are cold, label them, and make sure the lids are firmly screwed on. Store in a cool, dark place.

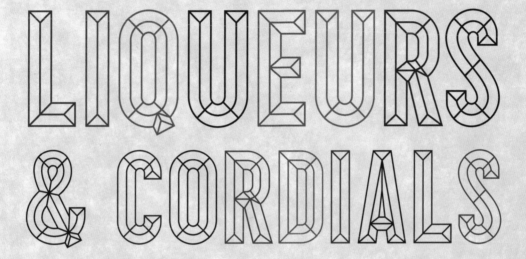

LIQUEURS & CORDIALS

Perfect Liqueurs & Cordials

Making flavoured drinks at home is not as difficult as you might imagine, and the results are spectacular. This chapter covers both the alcoholic versions, and those that the whole family can enjoy. The methods vary – sometimes the flavourings are cooked, sometimes they are raw – but the mission is the same: to produce a full-flavoured drink that tastes delicious, adds a new dimension to your store-cupboard, and makes an imaginative change from commercial alternatives.

Liqueurs

I find the strange thing about liqueurs is the dichotomy between the bought and the home-made. If you searched in the back of the cupboard where I keep my bottles of spirits and oddities, you would come across several half-used bottles of commercially made liqueurs: they sit there waiting, waiting, hoping presumably, that there will come a day when I need a little dash of this or glass of that. In contrast my home-made liqueurs vanish almost before my eyes.

It seems that when I offer them to people and mention that they are home-made, this makes after-dinner drinking more acceptable. And, once you've tasted home-made sloe gin or cranberry vodka, you're hooked.

A FEW THINGS TO KNOW ABOUT MAKING LIQUEURS

It is the purity of the ingredients that makes these drinks so good: just fruit, sugar and your chosen spirit. The basic recipe is simple: prepare your chosen flavouring, add this to the spirit, mix in the sugar and wait. That said, these recipes will all differ slightly in technique as I have found the individual liqueurs taste better with these slightly different methods.

★ I use both gin and vodka, looking for brands that have 40% alcohol. (A cheap own-brand supermarket one is fine.) This high percentage is not to give a bigger kick to the finished liqueur, but because the higher the alcohol level a spirit has, the more it holds the aromatics that you are adding.

★ Gin will already contain some aromatics so it is the best base for complex flavours such as those from wild fruit like sloes or blackberries.

★ Vodka on the other hand is a very clean-tasting spirit, and so is perfect for strawberries, cherries or as a base for spiced cranberry vodka.

★ Although I don't use it in the recipes here, brandy is good with orange flavours and with stone fruit like peaches.

★ Be sure to keep the original bottle or bottles in a safe place to return your liqueur to when it's ready. Alternatively, you can buy pretty glass bottles with china stoppers and rubber washers, and divide the liqueur between a couple of them. This makes a nice present, or you could take one as an offering at a party instead of wine.

★ Most fruit, if it has a distinct flavour and perfume, is suitable for making liqueurs at home. Some of my favourites are blackcurrant, raspberry, strawberry, cranberry and cherry.

★ It is best here to use white sugar, so once again I am using white granulated sugar. It is inexpensive, and will add nothing but the requisite sweetness to the drinks.

★ For the steeping process I either use a heavy food-safe plastic tub with a tight-fitting lid, or a large glass or china jug or bowl. Always cover the bowl or jug with a double layer of clingfilm to minimise evaporation, known in France as 'the angels' share'. For some liqueurs I use a deep, lidded glass jar.

★ Keep everything spotlessly clean – the container, bowl or jug, the bottles, even the muslin or cloth that you sieve the flavoured spirit through.

★ To sterilise or scald the cloth, make sure first that it is clean. Place it in a saucepan, cover with water, and bring to the boil. Simmer for 5 minutes, then drain. You can also wash the cloth in a washing machine, then, to sterilise it further, iron it with a hot iron, which will kill any lingering bacteria. You could use a paper coffee filter instead of cloth.

★ Scrub all bottles out well using a bottle brush and hot soapy water, then rinse in several changes of clean water. Lay the bottles on a baking tray or directly on the oven shelf and heat through for 20 minutes in an oven preheated to 100ºC/200ºF/Gas 2. Cool before using. Metal lids can be boiled for 5 minutes in a pan of water.

★ Alternatively, bottles and rubber seals can be sterilised using a solution such as Milton, following the instructions on the packaging.

★ It may be necessary to have a sterilised jar for any excess, but I usually find evaporation and tasting takes care of that.

★ If you intend to serve your liqueur frozen, be sure to use a heavy-duty bottle with a screw cap, and don't over-fill it. Liquid expands as it freezes and whilst the liqueur will be gelid, not solid, it will still need space in the bottle.

★ Once the liqueurs are bottled, store them in a cold, dark cupboard. I have found that those with fresh tastes like strawberry and raspberry are best drunk within the year, but sloe gin and cherry vodka keep getting better, and can be drunk several years after making, should they last that long!

How to Make the Perfect Bottle of Sloe Gin

The blackthorn bush grows rampantly in our hedgerows and gives much pleasure when it flowers, turning the field's edge into bridal lace. After this rather showy start the bush settles down to simply do the traditional job it was planted for: defining boundaries and keeping stock safe. It is only in late autumn that blackthorn comes back to our notice, because it is then that the canny walker will pick its fruit to make all manner of preserves, most notably sloe gin.

Tradition has it that sloes should be picked after the first frost, but sometimes tradition can be too proscriptive and make no sense. Frosts, in the south at least, seldom occur much before December, and if you leave picking your sloes until then, less hidebound foragers will have beaten you to it.

I think the frost imperative was to make the infusing of the sloes easier, as once the sloes freeze they expand and the skins crack. So I usually freeze them before steeping. I simply pick them as late as I can to allow them to swell and ripen, and then freeze them for anything from a week to a year. As the sloes thaw, the skins split and all that's needed is a simple bash with a potato masher to open the fruit to let the infusing commence.

Yield approx. 600–700g | *Keeps* up to 2 years

Ingredients
500g sloes
750ml gin
100g white granulated sugar

Equipment
Scales and a measuring jug ★ Colander ★ Freezer bag(s) ★ Medium plastic container with lid (or large bowl or jug), washed and dried ★ Potato masher ★ Reserved gin bottle with cap/lid, washed and dried ★ Baking tray ★ Sieve ★ Bowl ★ Coffee filter or scalded muslin ★ Funnel ★ Labels

1. Pick over the sloes and wash thoroughly before tipping into a freezer bag and freezing for a week or up to a year. **2.** Take the bag from the freezer and tip the frozen fruit into a plastic container with a tight-fitting lid. This must be deep enough to take the sloes, gin and sugar. **3.** Once the sloes have thawed, bash them about a bit with a potato masher then add the gin and sugar, clip on the lid and put in a cool, dark place. Be sure to keep a bottle for later. **4.** Leave the gin for two to three months, shaking the container every few days. **5.** When ready to make the gin, place the clean bottle and its lid on a baking tray and then into the oven preheated to 100°C/200°F/Gas 2 for 20 minutes. Cool before using. **6.** Place a sieve over a bowl, and line it with either a coffee filter or a piece of scalded muslin. **7.** Strain the fruit through the sieve, allowing the liquid to drip into the bowl. Reserve both liquid and fruit. **8.** Pour the sloe-flavoured gin into the sterilised bottle – I use an ordinary funnel – and put on the lid, checking it is tight. Label the bottle. **9.** Store the gin in a cool, dark place for six months before drinking.

Christmas Cranberry & Orange Liqueur

As soon as the cranberries come into the shops in late November I make a small bottle of this to serve as a digestive in my tiny antique glasses that only come out once a year. The colour is brilliant enough to brighten any day, and the cranberries have a dry edge that is the perfect antidote to rich food. I store mine in the freezer so it is thick, almost gelid, when I pour it. It also makes a lovely cocktail when diluted with sparkling wine.

Cranberries are imported from Canada. Check them carefully, sometimes there will be a few rotten ones in the box. Scrub the oranges well to remove the thin wax coating the producers use to prolong their shelf-life. Whilst you can easily buy unwaxed lemons, I find it much harder to buy unwaxed oranges.

Yield **approx. 750 ml** | *Keeps* 1 year

450g cranberries
2 large navel or similar oranges
225g white granulated sugar
750ml 40% vodka

1 . Wash the cranberries and spread them on a clean tea-towel, picking them over and discarding any that are rotten or squashed. **2 .** Scrub the oranges well with a scourer and hot water to remove any wax. Dry them. Now grate off all the zest using a fine Microplane grater. Use the flesh in another recipe. **3 .** Place the cranberries and sugar in a food processor or blender and whizz until the berries are finely chopped. **4 .** Transfer the mixture to a spotlessly clean glass or china bowl, stir in the orange zest and pour over the vodka. Be sure to keep a bottle plus the lid for later. **5 .** Stir again and cover the bowl carefully with a double layer of clingfilm. Place the bowl in a cool dark place and leave for three to four weeks. **6 .** Once a week for 4 weeks, stir the mixture with a sterilised metal spoon, re-covering the bowl carefully. **7 .** When you are ready to make the liqueur, place the reserved clean bottle on a baking tray, then into an oven preheated to 100°C/200°F/Gas 2 for 20 minutes. Cool before using. **8 .** Place a piece of scalded muslin or a coffee filter in a sieve and place the sieve over a clean bowl or wide jug. **9 .** Strain the liqueur mixture through the muslin into the bowl or jug, discarding the solids. **10 .** Pour the liqueur into the reserved and sterilised vodka bottle, using a funnel, and screw on the lid. Label the bottle. **11 .** Store in the freezer until needed. It can be drunk after three weeks.

Coffee Liqueur

This rich coffee liqueur would be equally at home poured over ice-cream or made into a seriously delicious espresso martini.

Vodka is my spirit of choice as it has a clean flavour and is readily available in half bottles. Choose one that has 40% alcohol as this level will best hold the aromatics you add, in this case the ground coffee. Grinding your own beans will ensure none of the essential oils that give this liqueur its amazing depth of flavour are lost. I used white sugar, but a lightly coloured, unrefined sugar would give another layer of flavour.

Leaving the spirit for two to three weeks allows a slow, cold transfer of flavour that gives the best result. You must cover the bowl or jug well to avoid the alcohol evaporating, but, inevitably, you will always lose some.

In this particular instance, it's essential that you line your sieve with a coffee filter or muslin to make sure the liqueur is not gritty.

Yield **approx. 350ml** | *Keeps* **up to 2 years**

375ml 40% vodka
100g white granulated sugar
60g chosen coffee beans

1 . Pour the vodka into a spotlessly clean jug or a bowl, and add the sugar. Be sure to keep the bottle plus the lid for later. **2 .** Grind the beans and add to the jug or bowl. Stir well and carefully cover with a double layer of clingfilm. **3 .** Place in a cold dark place for three weeks. Shake the jug or bowl from time to time to mix the ingredients together. **4 .** When you are ready to make the liqueur, place the reserved clean bottle on a baking tray, then into an oven preheated to 100°C/200°F/Gas 2 for 20 minutes. Cool before using. **5 .** Line a sieve with scalded muslin or a coffee filter, and place this over a clean jug. **6 .** Strain the liqueur through the sieve into the jug. Discard the coffee grounds. **7 .** Pour the coffee liqueur back into the reserved, sterilised bottle – I use an ordinary funnel – and screw on the lid. Label the bottle. **8 .** Store in a cool, dark place for three weeks before drinking.

Carla's Cherry Vodka

This delicious recipe comes from my friend Carla Tomasi, an Italian chef whom I've had the delight of working with on occasions. Carla now lives in Rome and tantalises me with stories of hot summers, long lazy meals and her wonderful home cooking.

She makes several bottles of this flavoured vodka early each summer as soon as the big reddish-black cherries come into the markets. I used frozen black sweet cherries and some dried sour Morello cherries to add complexity.

Carla has one last trick up her sleeve: once the vodka has infused for six weeks, she adds a shot or two of maple syrup. I've not tried this yet but intend to when I make my next batch.

I infuse the vodka in a large screw-top jar and then simply pour out a glass from the jar when I want one, or spoon out the cherries to serve over ice-cream and pancakes. This way, with the alcohol and fruit remaining together, the flavour just keeps getting better.

Yield **approx. 1 litre** | *Keeps* **1 year**

700ml 40% proof vodka
350g black cherries
125g dried Morello cherries
200g white granulated sugar

1 . Put the vodka, cherries and sugar into a spotlessly clean, deep, lidded glass jar. **2 .** Cover with the lid and put in a cool, dark place, shaking the jar whenever you remember. **3 .** You can begin to use the vodka after six weeks, but it is wonderful after six months.

Cordials

Home-made cordials are delightful. They can be made with any number of fruits from the garden or market, and I have even made a delicious cordial from beetroot. Cordials have a myriad of uses: you can dilute them with chilled water, fizzy or flat; you can use them to make wonderful cocktails; and they can be added to fruit desserts of all types. I like to have them to offer as interesting non-alcoholic alternatives at parties and on picnics.

Cordials are essentially flavoured heavy sugar syrups made acidic with the addition of citric acid. There are no preservatives apart from the sugar and citric acid so they have a short shelf-life, and it is important that you make sure everything is as clean as possible, including your equipment.

The basic method involves choosing your flavours, cooking them if necessary, then adding either sugar or a sugar syrup that has been previously cooked. Usually the fruit is sieved to remove any pulp, seeds or skin to give a smooth, clean texture. This fruit can be used in smoothies or spooned over yoghurt.

I make cordials in small quantities as they can ferment or grow moulds. Neither is particularly harmful but using the drinks within four to six weeks is best.

A FEW THINGS TO KNOW ABOUT MAKING CORDIALS

★ Ideally the fruit you use for cordials will be full flavoured and acidic, with citrus fruits like lemon and oranges, rhubarb and blackcurrants being the most usual.

★ Strawberries and raspberries can make delicious drinks, but must have acid added.

★ Added acidity also helps keep the cordial fresh, and I use citric acid powder for this, and lemon juice.

★ I use white granulated sugar for my cordials. This must be fully dissolved before the mixture comes to the boil. Timings involved in dissolving sugar will vary, but you must check that the pan no longer feels gritty, and that there are no signs of sugar crystals on your wooden spoon before continuing with the recipe.

★ I store my cordials in glass bottles with metal-hinged glass or china stoppers sealed with a small rubber washer, as these can be easily heated to kill any bacteria.

★ You can use sterilised spirit bottles, but not empty wine bottles that are closed with corks, as these may carry yeasts that can cause the cordial to spoil. Thoroughly washed screw-topped wine bottles are fine.

★ Scrub all bottles out well using a bottle brush and hot soapy water, then rinse in several changes of clean water. Lay the bottles on a baking tray or directly on the oven shelf and heat through for 20 minutes in an oven preheated to 100°C/200°F/Gas 2. Cool before using. Metal lids can be boiled for 5 minutes in a pan of water.

★ Alternatively, bottles and rubber seals can be sterilised using a solution such as Milton, following the instructions on the packaging.

★ You should only use metal spoons when stirring cordials as wooden spoons can also carry mould spores and bacteria. These metal spoons can be sterilised in boiling water.

★ If you need to strain the cordial, first scald the muslin or jelly bag by placing it in a pan of boiling water and simmering for 2 minutes.

★ Once bottled, cordials are ready to be drunk.

★ Cordials should be stored in a cool, dark place, but if you've room in the fridge so much the better.

★ Some cordials do not keep well, so therefore as a rule of thumb, drink them up quickly.

How to Make the Perfect Bottle of Rhubarb Cordial

Early 'champagne' rhubarb gives this a lovely colour though you could use later unforced rhubarb, adding a few raspberries or some strawberries for both colour and flavour. To get the most flavour from the rhubarb, wash it then cook it slowly in a covered pan in just the water clinging to the skin.

This cordial is delicious diluted with either fizzy or flat water, makes a great champagne cocktail, and can be added to fruit salads and other fruit desserts.

Yield approx. 750 ml | *Keeps* 3 weeks

Ingredients

1kg fresh rhubarb
approx. 600g white granulated sugar (100g sugar for each 100ml strained juice)
1 teaspoon citric acid powder for each 200g sugar

Equipment

Scales and measuring jug ★ Some glass bottles with screw-on or hinged lids, washed and dried ★ Baking tray ★ Chopping board and knife ★ Colander ★ Heavy-bottomed saucepan with a lid ★ Fine sieve ★ Muslin square ★ Glass jug ★ Metal spoon ★ Funnel ★ Label

1. Place some clean bottles and their lids on a baking tray and then into the oven preheated to 100°C/200°F/Gas 2 for 20 minutes. **2.** Trim the rhubarb, and cut into 5cm pieces. Place these in a colander and wash well. **3.** Now put the rhubarb into a pan and put on the lid. Cook the rhubarb over a very low heat until it collapses and stews. This will take about 10 minutes. **4.** Line a sieve with scalded muslin, and place over a spotlessly clean glass jug. Strain the juice from the rhubarb through the sieve into the jug. You will have about 400-600ml juice. (The rhubarb flesh can be saved and eaten on yoghurt or ice-cream.) **5.** Pour the juice back into a clean saucepan, and add the measured amount of sugar – 100g per 100ml juice – stirring with a clean metal spoon. **6.** Put the pan over a low heat and simmer, stirring, until the sugar has fully dissolved, and there is no grittiness either on the spoon or in the pan. **7.** Turn up the heat and bring the syrup to the boil. Boil the syrup, uncovered, for 5 minutes. **8.** Turn off the heat, stir in the citric acid until fully dissolved, and leave the cordial for 5 minutes. Take the baking tray of bottles from oven at the same time. **9.** Pour the cordial into the hot bottles, using a funnel, and seal with the lids. Label the bottle clearly. **10.** Store in the fridge. The cordial can be drunk straightaway.

Blood Orange Cordial

Blood oranges come into the shops in early January so that is the time to make this cordial. If you can, buy fruits that are really red when cut open, as this will give the best colour to your cordial.

Infusing the zest in the syrup for a few days makes sure you get every ounce of flavour into your cordial.

Yield **approx. 1 litre** | *Keeps* **3 months**

6 blood oranges
400ml water
600ml white granulated sugar
40g citric acid powder

1 . Begin by scrubbing the oranges in hot water, using a vegetable brush or scourer, to remove any wax on the skins. **2** . Using a fine grater, grate all the zest from the oranges into a large, spotlessly clean glass bowl or jug. **3** . Squeeze the juice from the oranges and add this to the zest. **4** . Measure the water and sugar into a heavy-based pan and place over a low heat. **5** . Simmer, stirring, until the sugar has completely dissolved and there is no grittiness either in the pan or on the spoon. **6** . Turn up the heat and boil the syrup, uncovered, for 5 minutes. **7** . Stir the citric acid into the hot syrup and then pour this into the juice and zest mixture. Stir. **8** . Cover the bowl with a double layer of clingfilm and put the bowl in a cool dark place for four days. Shake from time to time. **9** . Place some clean glass bottles and their lids on a baking tray and then into the oven preheated to 100°C/200°F/Gas 2 for 20 minutes. Cool before using. **10** . Line a sieve with scalded muslin and place over a spotlessly clean large, wide-mouthed jug. Strain the cordial through the sieve into the jug. Take the baking tray of bottles from the oven. **11** . Pour the cordial into the cold sterilised bottles, and seal with the lids. Label the bottles. **12** . Store in a cool, dark place. The cordial can be drunk straightaway.

Blackcurrant Cordial

A real children's favourite, this. Blackcurrants are full of vitamin C, so it could be said to be good for them but, as ever, fruit cordials are packed with sugar so do dilute it well with chilled water or, for a grown-up taste of summer, chilled white wine. In winter this makes a wonderfully warming drink when diluted with hot water.

Pick the blackcurrants over before you make the cordial and wash them well as they can be very dusty.

Yield **approx. 2 litres** | *Keeps* **4-6 weeks**

750g blackcurrants
1.5 litres water
1kg white granulated sugar
2 teaspoons citric acid powder

1 . Begin by checking the fruit over and discarding any squashed or mouldy berries. **2 .** Wash the berries well under a running cold tap then put them into a deep, heavy-bottomed saucepan with the measured water. **3 .** Place the pan over a medium heat, cover with the lid, and bring to a simmer. **4 .** Place some clean glass bottles and their lids on a baking tray and then into the oven preheated to 100°C/200°F/Gas 2 to heat through gently. Cool before using. **5 .** Cook the berries for 10 minutes, then strain the juice through a fine sieve into a clean pan. You can press down on the fruit to make sure you get the maximum amount of flavour. **6 .** Put the sugar into the pan along with the juice, and return the pan to the heat. Stir until the sugar has completely dissolved and there is no grittiness either in the pan or on the spoon. **7 .** Bring the mixture to the boil and simmer, uncovered, for 2 minutes before stirring in the citric acid. Take the baking tray of bottles from the oven. **8 .** Pour the hot cordial through a funnel into the hot bottles, put on the lids and leave to cool. Label the bottles. **9 .** Store in a cool, dark place, preferably the fridge. The cordial can be drunk straightaway.

Mint Syrup

A short and simple recipe this, but a useful one nevertheless. Make the syrup when you have a flush of new young mint ready for use later in the summer.

I use the syrup poured over strawberries. The combination works beautifully, and if you've not tried it, you should. It makes a refreshing drink and sometime I dilute it with hot water to warm a late summer night.

Take care as you pick the mint. Try and cut it cleanly, avoiding any soil contamination, and do pick lots; it grows better if harvested regularly.

Yield **approx. 600ml** | *Keeps* **4–6 weeks**

500g white granulated sugar
650ml water
a colanderful of fresh mint, 3 x supermarket
  packets, 100g in total
30g citric acid powder

1 . Place the sugar and water into a heavy-bottomed pan and place over a low heat. Simmer, stirring, until the sugar has completely dissolved and there is no grittiness either in the pan or on the spoon. **2 .** Turn up the heat and bring the syrup to a boil. Boil, uncovered, for 5 minutes. **3 .** Meanwhile wash the mint and shake it dry. Chop it roughly and add to the syrup. Boil for a further minute then turn off the heat, and add the citric acid, stirring until it has dissolved. **4 .** Cover the pan, and leave the syrup to infuse for 12–24 hours. Shake the bowl from time to time. **5 .** When you are ready to make the syrup, place some clean glass bottles and their lids on a baking tray and then into the oven preheated to 100°C/200°F/Gas 2 for 20 minutes. Cool before using. **6 .** Line a sieve with scalded muslin and place over a spotlessly clean large, wide-mouthed jug. Strain the cordial through the sieve into the jug. Take the baking tray of bottles from the oven. **7 .** Pour the cordial into the cold bottles, and put on the lids. Label the bottles. **8 .** Store in a cool, dark place. The mint syrup can be used straightaway.

Strawberry Cordial

This is a lovely pink drink that would make a perfect way to refresh you and your guests at a summer picnic. You can dilute it with chilled water or fizzy wine, and both will taste special. I like to add it to pitchers of white sangria or splash a little into fruit salads.

Choose firm, ripe but not mushy strawberries. This is the time to use the most fragrant variety you can find, as it is that elusive perfume that you are trying to capture in the syrup. Never use any part of a mouldy strawberry, as it will taint the cordial and increase its chance of fermenting.

Cordials are prone to ferment anyway, and here fresh yeasts on the barely cooked berries love the syrupy mix, so do take care to make sure all the equipment you use is spotlessly clean.

Yield **approx. 1 litre** | *Keeps* **4 weeks**

500g strawberries
500ml water
750g white granulated sugar
50g citric acid powder

1. Begin by preparing the strawberries: wash the fruit well and remove the stalks. Dry them gently on kitchen paper. **2.** Now place them in a clean glass or china bowl and mash them with a clean metal fork. **3.** Place the water and sugar in a heavy-bottomed pan and put this over a low heat. Stir with a metal spoon until the sugar has completely dissolved and there is no grittiness either in the pan or on the spoon. **4.** Bring the syrup to the boil, then simmer for 5 minutes, uncovered, before stirring in the citric acid. **5.** Pour the boiling syrup over the fruit in the bowl and stir well, using a clean metal spoon. **6.** Cover the bowl with a double layer of clingfilm and let the contents cool. **7.** Put the bowl into the fridge and leave to allow the flavours to infuse for 24 hours. Shake from time to time. **8.** When you are ready to make the cordial, place some clean glass bottles and their lids on a baking tray and then into the oven preheated to 100°C/200°F/Gas 2 for 20 minutes. Cool before using. **9.** Line a sieve with scalded muslin and place over a spotlessly clean large, wide-mouthed jug. Strain the cordial through the sieve into the jug. Take the baking tray of bottles from the oven. **10.** Pour the cordial into the cold sterilised bottles, and put on the lids. Label the bottles. **11.** Store in a cool, dark place, preferably the fridge. The cordial can be drunk straightaway.

Christmas Cordial

There are many reasons why you may want to choose a non-alcoholic drink, especially at Christmas, when the delight of being invited to parties is tempered by the worry over what it is wise to drink. Fruit juices are fine, as are fizzy mixers, but something a little more complex would be lovely.

I make big jugs of this cordial for parties, diluting it with still or fizzy water and adding cucumber slices to one pitcher and sliced oranges and lemons to the other.

Make sure you use spotlessly clean equipment, metal spoons and glass bottles to minimise the risk of the cordial fermenting.

Yield approx. 750 ml | *Keeps* 4 weeks

2 limes
300g white granulated sugar
750ml water
60g fresh root ginger
1 x 10cm cinnamon stick
1 tablespoon cardamom pods

1 . Scrub the limes under a hot tap to remove any wax, dust or mould spores. Then chop the fruit roughly. **2 .** Put the sugar and water into a heavy-bottomed pan and then put this over a low heat. **3 .** Simmer, stirring, until the sugar has completely dissolved, and there is no grittiness either in the pan or on the spoon. **4 .** Turn up the heat and boil the syrup, uncovered, for 5 minutes. **5 .** Roughly grate the fresh ginger. Crush the whole spices in a mortar, using a pestle, until roughly ground. **6 .** Tip the spices and the chopped limes into the hot syrup, then return this just to boiling point. **7 .** Turn off the heat and cover the pan with the lid. Leave to infuse for 24 hours. **8 .** When you are ready to make the cordial, place some clean glass bottles and their lids on a baking tray and then into the oven preheated to 100°C/200°F/Gas 2 to heat through gently for 20 minutes. Cool before using. **9 .** Line a sieve with scalded muslin and place over a spotlessly clean large, wide-mouthed jug. Strain the cordial through the sieve into the jug. Take the baking tray of bottles from the oven. **10 .** Pour the cordial into the cold sterilised bottles, and put on the lids. Label the bottles. **11 .** Store in a cool, dark place. The cordial can be drunk straightaway.

Elderflower Cordial

As a child, foraging hedgerows and meadows was an integral part of life, the seasons punctuated by what we gathered. 'Food for free' in those days supplemented our limited post-war diet and gave us hours of exercise and fresh air. Today foraging is very much the vogue, so here is the first recipe in my yearly foraging calendar.

Huge heady elderflowers adorn the hedgerows, usually appearing in late May, though this will depend on the type of spring we are having. Elderflowers are highly scented, and it is this scent that you are trying to capture in the cordial. Pick them early on a dry morning and choose ones that are just open, not the overblown pollen-dusted ones. Shake them gently to dislodge any insect life, and be sure to choose those from at least waist-level to avoid any that might have had the attention of passing dogs.

Use the cordial diluted with chilled fizzy and still water or sparkling wine. It's lovely added to summer wine cups, and to the syrup for fruit salads on page 133.

Yield approx. 2 litres | *Keeps* up to 4 months

2 lemons
2 oranges
4 limes
20–30 large elderflower heads
1kg white granulated sugar
1.5 litres water
60g citric acid powder

1 . Begin by scrubbing the fruit well under hot water, using a vegetable brush or scourer, to remove any wax coating. Chop it into 2cm cubes. **2 .** Put the fruit into a large spotlessly clean glass or china bowl with the flowers. You could also use a heavy food-safe plastic tub with a tight-fitting lid. **3 .** Put the sugar and water into a heavy-bottomed pan and then put this over a low heat. **4 .** Simmer, stirring, until the sugar has competely dissolved and there is no grittiness either in the pan or on the spoon. **5 .** Turn up the heat and bring the syrup to the boil. Boil, uncovered, for 5 minutes, then stir in the citric acid. **6 .** Pour the hot syrup over the fruit and flowers. Stir with a clean metal spoon and then cover with a double layer of clingfilm (or the lid). **7 .** Place the container in a cool dark place to infuse for four days. If you have room, the fridge is ideal, but if not, the coldest place you have. Stir daily, using a fresh clean spoon each time. **8 .** When you are ready to make the cordial, place some clean glass bottles and their lids on a baking tray and then into the oven preheated to 100°C/200°F/Gas 2 for 20 minutes. Cool before using. **9 .** Line a sieve with a piece of scalded muslin and place over a spotlessly clean large, wide-mouthed jug. Strain the cordial through the sieve into the jug. Take the baking tray of bottles from the oven. **10 .** Pour the cordial into the cold sterilised bottles, and put on the lids. Label the bottles. **12 .** Store in a cool, dark place. The cordial can be drunk straightaway.

Perfect Fruit Butters and Cheeses

Fruit butters and cheese are grouped together here rather than with the fruit curds, as they have much in common. Both are made from fruit that is plentiful, both are cooked to a smooth purée, neither contain dairy products, but from there on they differ.

Fruit butters have been an important part of the European table for many centuries. They originated in Germany and the Netherlands from whence they travelled to America. Fruit butters have a smooth light consistency, ideal for topping pancakes or waffles, spreading on bread, toast or cakes, and spooning into natural yoghurt.

Fruit cheeses have been popular for many centuries throughout Europe, where these thick, rich, firmly set jellies, being easily portable, were served to supplement picnics and food eaten by travellers. They are a close relation of fruit comfits and sugar-dusted fruit-jelly sweetmeats, which were popular on medieval tables.

Fruit cheeses are usually made with pectin-rich fruit, and cooked until the purée is very thick, when they can be set in a mould and sliced. Fruit cheeses are wonderful on a winter cheese-board.

Fruit Butters

'Fruit butter' is a slight misnomer as there is no butter, cream or even milk used in its making.

The word 'butter' is actually a reference to the texture of this thick, rich and smooth spread.

A FEW THINGS TO KNOW ABOUT MAKING FRUIT BUTTERS

★ These butters are an excellent way of making best use of a glut of fruit or some of the sweeter vegetables like carrot, pumpkin or sweet potato.

★ The fruit or vegetables are washed and chopped up with any blemishes cut away, then cooked until they are very soft.

★ The soft fruit or vegetables are rubbed through a fine sieve to remove any skins, cores and pips, which are discarded. The resulting purée is then returned to a clean heavy-bottomed pan and cooked slowly until thick before the sugar is added. I use my heavy, non-reactive preserving pan.

★ It is very important to stir thoroughly and often as the purée thickens, as it has a tendency to catch. I find it best to use a flat-bottomed wooden spatula to stir and scrape the pan.

★ Be careful when the purée is reducing, as the bubbles are somewhat volcanic. I use a splatter guard at this stage to trap the hot mixture.

★ When making fruit butter, you might have to use a heat diffuser if you can't get your hob to a low enough setting.

★ Reducing the purée down before the sugar goes in allows you to use less sugar to sweeten your preserve. Do remember though that sugar is a preservative, so the lower the amount of sugar the shorter the shelf-life. I usually use white granulated sugar in my fruit butters.

★ I have given the minimum amount of sugar I would use in my recipes. If you wish to store the butters in a pantry, you should add double the quantities in the recipes. The master recipe on page 142 will give you an idea.

★ Whatever sugar you use, or how much of it, it must be fully dissolved in your preserve before you continue with the recipe. Timings involved in dissolving sugar will vary, according to sugar type, heat of liquid etc. You must check that the pan no longer feels gritty, and that there are no signs of sugar crystals on your wooden spoon.

★ Fruit butters do not rely on pectin to help them set, but they are best made either with fruit that has some substance such as apples, pears or quince, or a mix of fruits like strawberry and rhubarb.

★ For the browner butters – apple, pumpkin, carrot etc. – I use raw sugar, either light or dark brown, as the richer flavour of these sugars really works well here.

★ To check whether a butter is ready, lift up a large spoonful. If the butter runs over the side of the spoon when held level, cook for a little longer. If the purée forms a mound on the spoon, you can stop cooking, as it is ready.

★ All jars must be spotlessly clean and sterilised in a low oven before use. Put them and their lids on a baking tray and into the oven preheated to 100ºC/200ºF/Gas 2 to heat gently for 20 minutes.

★ Try and grind your spices when you need them, or buy them ready-ground in small quantities and use them up quickly. That way they will keep their flavour.

★ Store the butters in a cool, dark place. If your butter has a low-sugar content, it will have to be stored in the fridge.

How to Make the Perfect Jar of Spiced Apple Butter

I find apple butter very handy indeed. It can be served as a spread on toast, offered with Sunday's roast pork, and even stirred into gravies and sauces to add a fruity base note. As this butter has a high content of sugar, it can be kept for a year.

Yield approx. 2kg | *Keeps* 1 year

Ingredients

2kg apples, cooking or eating
6 cloves
$\frac{1}{2}$ nutmeg
1 x 10cm cinnamon stick
80g fresh root ginger, peeled
650ml water
600g–1kg white granulated sugar

Equipment

Scales and a measuring jug ★ Colander ★ Chopping board and sharp knife ★ Pestle and mortar (or rolling pin and heavy bowl) ★ Large heavy-bottomed, non-reactive preserving pan with a lid ★ Sieve ★ Wooden spoon and spatula ★ Splatter guard ★ Some glass jars with lids, washed and dried ★ Baking tray ★ Heat diffuser if necessary ★ Jam funnel or metal ladle ★ Labels

1. Wash the fruit well in a colander under cold running water then cut the apples into large chunks removing any bruises and blemishes.
2. Using a pestle and mortar or a rolling pin and heavy bowl, crush the cloves, nutmeg and cinnamon. Roughly chop the peeled ginger.
3. Now put the ginger and spices, along with the apples and water, into a heavy-bottomed pan.

4. Place the pan over a moderate heat and bring to a simmer. Cover and cook for 30 minutes until the apples are very soft. **5.** Allow the fruit to cool a little then rub it through a fine sieve, using a wooden spoon. Weigh the purée and return it to the washed pan. **6.** Now put the pan back on the heat and simmer to reduce the purée by half, about 30 minutes. **7.** Stir in the sugar, adding at least 650g for up to 1kg, per kg of purée, or 65–100g per 100g purée. The more sugar you add, the longer your butter will last. **8.** Stir constantly with a wooden spoon, still over a low heat, until the sugar has completely dissolved: the mixture should not feel gritty when stirred, and there should be no signs of sugar on the back of your spoon. **9.** Continue to cook the butter, for at least another 30 minutes, until it is very thick. Be careful, the bubbles are somewhat volcanic. You may need a splatter guard and a spatula to stir and scrape the pan. **10.** Meanwhile, place some clean jam jars and their lids on a baking tray and then into the oven preheated to 100°C/200°F/Gas 2 for 20 minutes. **11.** The purée will become darker in colour as it thickens. You may need to place the pan on a heat diffuser to prevent the purée from sticking and so burning. **12.** To check whether the butter is ready, lift up a large spoonful. If the butter runs over the side of the spoon when held level, cook for a little longer. If the purée forms a mound on the spoon, you can stop cooking, as it is ready. Take the baking tray of jars from the oven. **13.** Pot the butter into the hot jars. I use a jam funnel to help with this, but a ladle is fine. Top with the lids. **14.** When cold, label and check the lids are firmly screwed on. Store in a cool, dark place.

Rhubarb & Strawberry Butter

Some matches are made in heaven, at least that part of heaven reserved for taste and flavour: lamb and mint, cinnamon and apple….But of all such matches, I think the harmony of rhubarb and strawberry one of the finest. Their flavours apart I enjoy, but put together they create something sublime.

Early spring sees the advent of lovely, fine champagne rhubarb. This forced, pale pink rhubarb is a real treat. It comes from the 'Rhubarb Triangle' in Yorkshire where the plants are 'forced' in dark sheds so no chlorophyll forms in the tender stems. This really is the king of rhubarb and is available only for a short time.

Alongside the rhubarb in early spring we get the first imported strawberries, and whilst they are not to my taste, they do make a lovely fruit butter when mixed with the rhubarb.

Naturally this preserve can be made with wonderful home-grown produce in early summer. You can force your rhubarb by covering the plants with a bucket or similar to keep out the light. However, whilst I prefer forced rhubarb in this preserve, any tender young rhubarb will do.

This is a low-sugar preserve and so has a shorter shelf-life than some other fruit butters.

Yield **approx. 1.5kg** | *Keeps* **6 weeks**

1kg tender rhubarb
1kg strawberries
400g white granulated sugar

1 . Cut the rhubarb into 2.5cm pieces and place in a pan. I use a wide, deep sauté pan for this preserve. **2 .** Now hull the strawberries and put them into a blender. Whizz until you have a purée. **3 .** Pour the strawberry purée into the pan along with the rhubarb and add the sugar. **4 .** Stir constantly with a wooden spoon, still over a low heat, until the sugar has completely dissolved: the mixture should not feel gritty when stirred, and there should be no signs of sugar on the back of your spoon. **5 .** Now turn up the heat and cook at a slow boil, again stirring often, for about 35–45 minutes. By this time the butter will be thick and creamy, the rhubarb collapsed. **6 .** Turn off the heat and leave the butter to rest for 10 minutes. **7 .** Meanwhile, place some clean jam jars and their lids on a baking tray and then into the oven preheated to 100°C/200°F/Gas 2 to heat through gently for 20 minutes. **8 .** When the butter is cooled a little, taste it and check it's sweet enough. This is a personal thing, so add extra sugar to taste, then stir well to make sure it has completely dissolved. **9 .** Return the pan to the heat and bring back to the boil. Cook, stirring often, until you have a thick purée. **10 .** To check whether the butter is ready, lift up a large spoonful. If the butter runs over the side of the spoon when held level, cook for a little longer. If the purée forms a mound on the spoon, you can stop cooking, as it is ready. Take the baking tray of jars from the oven. **11 .** Pot the butter into the hot jars. I use a jam funnel to help with this, but a ladle is fine. Top with the lids. **12 .** When the jars are cold, label them, and check the lids are firmly screwed on. Store in the fridge.

Spiced Pumpkin & Maple Butter

I first ate this when travelling in North America, where pumpkin is used as often in desserts as it is as a vegetable. The colour of the finished butter is quite beautiful, and the flavour rich and deep. Try if you can to get real maple syrup and add this at the end of cooking.

This butter can be spread on toast, piled on to fruit loaf or, best yet, spooned on to breakfast pancakes or waffles and topped with whipped cream.

As pumpkin is quite dense I find it best to steam it before I purée it. You could also bake it in a low oven until soft.

Rather than the Halloween-style pumpkin, I prefer to use one with a denser flesh. My favourite is Crown Prince, a beautiful-looking winter squash with a silver-grey skin and deep orange flesh.

Yield **approx. 1.3kg** | *Keeps* **6 months**

2kg raw pumpkin, prepared weight

600g raw light brown sugar

1 x 20cm cinnamon stick or 1 tablespoon
   ground cinnamon

½ nutmeg, freshly grated, or 1 teaspoon
   ground nutmeg

2 large lemons

100ml maple syrup

1 . Prepare the pumpkin by carefully peeling it with a sharp knife and then removing any seeds. I scrape these out with a dessertspoon. Cut the flesh into 5cm cubes. **2 .** Cook the pumpkin. Either place it in a baking dish with a teacup of water, cover with a foil lid and bake in a low oven at 150°C/300°F/Gas 3 for 45 minutes or until soft, or cook in a steamer until soft. **3 .** Once the pumpkin is cooked, whizz it in a blender or food processer to give you a purée. **4 .** Scrape this purée into a preserving pan and add the sugar. **5 .** Using a coffee mill, grind the whole spices to a fine powder. Wash and dry the lemons, then finely grate the zest, and squeeze the juice. Stir the spices plus the lemon juice and zest into the mixture. **6 .** Meanwhile, place some clean jam jars and their lids on a baking tray and then into the oven preheated to 100ºC/200ºF/Gas 2 for 20 minutes. **7 .** Place the pan on a low heat, and stir constantly with a wooden spoon, still over a low heat, until the sugar has completely dissolved: the mixture should not feel gritty when stirred, and there should be no signs of sugar on the back of your spoon. **8 .** Now bring to a simmer and cook the purée, stirring often with the wooden spoon, until the mixture is very thick, about 15–20 minutes. **9 .** To check whether the butter is ready, lift up a large spoonful. If the butter runs over the side of the spoon when held level, cook for a little longer. If the purée forms a mound on the spoon, you can stop cooking, as it is ready. **10 .** When the purée is very thick and ready, stir in the maple syrup. Take the baking tray of jars from the oven. **11 .** Pot the butter into the hot jars. I use a jam funnel to help with this, but a ladle is fine. Top with the lids. **12 .** When the jars are cold, label them, and check the lids are firmly screwed on. Store in a cool, dark place.

Blueberry Lime Butter

When I lived in Suffolk, a blueberry grower planted a few hundred bushes on the sandy soil and soon started gathering quite a decent crop. I was delighted by this, as I'd learned to love blueberries when I lived in New York, so having a local supply was very good news.

Blueberries contain almost no pectin so I had to use some apple when making the jam on page 47. Fruit butters don't rely on a set in the way jams do, so this is the perfect recipe for those big bags of unsorted blueberries I used to buy from the gate.

I'm not sieving this butter, but feel free to do so if you want a totally smooth preserve.

Yield **approx. 900g** | *Keeps* **4 months**

1kg blueberries
juice of 2 limes
400g white granulated sugar
½ teaspoon finely ground coriander seeds

1. Wash the blueberries under cold running water then pick them over, discarding any squashed or mouldy ones. **2.** Tip the berries into a large heavy-bottomed pan, with just the water on them, cover with a lid and cook over a low heat, shaking the pan from time to time, until the berries pop and soften. This will take about 10 minutes. **3.** Scrape the berries into a liquidiser and whizz until very smooth. Return to the pan. Alternatively use a stick blender, directly in the pan. **4.** Now stir in the lime juice, sugar and ground coriander, and cook the butter over a low heat. Stir constantly with a wooden spoon until the sugar has completely dissolved: the mixture should not feel gritty when stirred, and there should be no signs of sugar on the back of your spoon. **5.** Continue to cook the butter, stirring from time to time, until the mixture is very thick. This will take about 45 minutes to an hour. I find the best tool to use for stirring the thick butter is a flat-ended wooden spatula, as this makes scraping the bottom and sides of the pan easier. **6.** Meanwhile, place some clean jam jars and their lids on a baking tray and then into the oven preheated to 100°C/200°F/Gas 2 for 20 minutes. **7.** To check whether the butter is ready, lift up a large spoonful. If the butter runs over the side of the spoon when held level, cook for a little longer. If the purée forms a mound on the spoon, you can stop cooking, as it is ready. Take the baking tray of jars from the oven. **8.** Pot into the hot jars. I use a jam funnel to help with this, but a ladle is fine. Top with the lids. **9.** When the jars are cold, label them, and check the lids are firmly screwed on. Store in a cool, dark place.

Cinnamon & Plum Butter

This plum butter is one I make often and keep in the fridge for my husband to spoon on to his breakfast yoghurt. I use only 300g of sugar, hence the necessity to store it in the fridge. Should you wish the preserve to be longer lasting, increase the sugar to 750g.

Yield **approx. 750g** | *Keeps* **6 weeks**

1kg large red or yellow plums
juice and zest of 2 large oranges
300g white granulated sugar
1 x 10cm cinnamon stick, finely ground

1. Wash the plums well under cold running water then, with a sharp knife, cut the plums in half. Remove and discard the stones. **2.** Cut the plum flesh into large pieces and place in a heavy-bottomed pan. **3.** Scrub the oranges well under hot water, using a vegetable brush or scourer, in order to remove any dust or wax. **4.** Using a Microplane or similar grater, grate the zest from the oranges then squeeze out the juice, adding both to the pan with the plums and the sugar. **5.** Place the pan over a moderate heat and bring to a simmer. Cover the pan and simmer for 20 minutes until the plums are very soft. **6.** Allow the purée to cool a little, then rub it through a sieve, using a wooden spoon, and return it to the washed pan. **7.** Now put the pan back on the heat and simmer to reduce the purée by half. This should take about 15–20 minutes. **8.** Stir constantly with a wooden spoon, still over a low heat, until the sugar has completely dissolved: the mixture should not feel gritty when stirred, and there should be no signs of sugar on the back of your spoon. **9.** Continue to cook the butter until it is very thick, about another 60 minutes. Be careful, the bubbles are somewhat volcanic. I use a splatter guard at this stage to trap the hot mixture. I also find it is best to use a flat-bottomed wooden spatula to stir and scrape the pan. **10.** Meanwhile, place some clean jam jars and their lids on a baking tray and then into the oven preheated to 100°C/200°F/Gas 2 for 20 minutes. **11.** To check whether the butter is ready, lift up a large spoonful. If the butter runs over the side of the spoon when held level, cook for a little longer. If the purée forms a mound on the spoon, you can stop cooking, as it is ready. Take the baking tray of jars from the oven. **12.** Pot the butter into the hot jars. I use a jam funnel to help with this, but a ladle is fine. Top with the lids. **13.** When the jars are cold, label them, and check the lids are firmly screwed on. Store in the fridge.

Fruit Cheeses

Fruit cheeses are in many ways similar to fruit butters in that they contain no dairy and are, at their simplest, single fruit purées cooked until very thick.

Whilst you can make fruit butter with almost any fruit, a fruit cheese needs pectin to give a sufficiently jellied finish that allows you to shape and slice the purée. Apples, plums and quinces are traditional fruit for making cheeses, but remember you can mix and match with other fruits to expand your choice of flavours.

It is traditional to set cheeses in moulds which are then turned out and can look very attractive on a cheese board.

A FEW THINGS TO KNOW ABOUT MAKING FRUIT CHEESES

★ As with most of the preserves in this book, I use white sugar when making fruit cheeses. Ensure the sugar is fully dissolved in your preserve before you continue with the recipe. Timings involved in dissolving sugar will vary, according to sugar type, heat of liquid etc. Check that the pan isn't gritty, and that there are no sugar crystals on your spoon.

★ Fruit cheeses can cook for a very long time. If you are worried about sticking, and you can't turn your heat low enough, you might have to use a heat diffuser. Towards the end of cooking, cheese mixtures have a tendency to stick to the bottom of the pan and to coat the sides. Use your spatula to scrape the sides and the base of the pan, and stir these thicker bits in well.

★ When it's thick enough to leave a clear channel when you drag the spatula through the bottom of the pan, it is ready to spoon into the moulds.

★ You can spoon the cheese into shallow disposable aluminium foil or plastic trays, or glass or china moulds. Small ramekins are ideal for this, but traditional china jelly moulds can be used for special-occasion fruit cheeses.

★ Cover the trays with lids and when cool store in a cool, dark place. Glass jars can be used and covered in the usual way. Cheeses in moulds that don't have lids must be covered with a double layer of clingfilm pressed down on to the surface of the cheese, to remove as much air as possible.

★ I usually pot up at least some of my cheese in hot jars, that have just been sterilised in an oven preheated to 100ºC/200ºF/Gas 2 for 20 minutes. I seal these jars with wax discs and cellophane. The cheese is then a sealed environment and thus keeps longer.

★ To unmould the cheese, let the mould sit in boiling water for a few moments, turn on to a plate, then give the mould a good shake. Moulded cheeses should be stored in the fridge and eaten within a month. Those made in trays or jars will last much longer, for up to a year.

How to Make the Perfect Quince Cheese

Quince cheese, known worldwide by its Spanish name, *membrillo*, was traditionally only served with Manchego, the matured sheep's milk cheese ubiquitous in tapas bars everywhere. These days, Spanish food is undergoing a renaissance, and *membrillo* can be found in many more dishes.

Fresh quinces can be large and very hard to cut, so do take care. And make sure the purée is thoroughly cooked before you continue with the recipe. There is no need to peel the quinces as you will sieve the purée later.

Yield approx. 1.3 kg | *Keeps* 1 year in jars or trays, 1 month in moulds

Ingredients
1kg large quinces
900g white granulated sugar
140ml fresh lemon juice

Equipment
Scales and a measuring jug ★ Colander ★ Chopping board and sharp knife ★ Large heavy-bottomed, non-reactive preserving pan with a lid ★ Blender or food processor ★ Sieve ★ Wooden spoon and flat spatula ★ Metal ladle ★ Aluminium trays, china or silicone moulds ★ Clingfilm ★ Labels

1 . Begin by washing the quinces in a colander under running water. Cut them into chunks of about 4cm. **2 .** Place the quince chunks in a deep heavy-bottomed pan and add enough water to just cover the fruit. **3 .** Place the pan over a moderate heat and bring to a simmer. Cover the pan and cook for 30–40 minutes until the quince is very soft. **4 .** Allow to cool a little, then strain off the water. Spoon the contents of the pan into a blender or food processor and whizz until smooth. Rub the purée through a fine sieve, discarding the fibrous solids that are left. Return the purée to the washed pan. **5 .** Add the sugar and lemon juice to the quince purée, then cook over a low heat, stirring often, until the sugar has completely dissolved: the mixture should not feel gritty when stirred, and there should be no signs of sugar on the back of your spoon. **6 .** Still keeping the heat low, and stirring often with your wooden spoon, cook the purée until it is very thick indeed, when it will become a deep red. This can take up to 2 hours. **7 .** Towards the end of cooking the mixture has a worrying tendency to stick to the bottom of the pan and to coat the sides. Use your wooden spatula to scrape both the sides and the base of the pan frequently, and stir these thicker bits in well. **8 .** When the paste is thick enough to leave a clear channel when you drag the spatula through the bottom of the pan, it is ready to spoon into the moulds. **9 .** Spoon the paste into your chosen flat trays or moulds and level the tops with a palette knife. **10 .** Put the moulds and trays somewhere cool to set. Cover the moulds with a double layer of clingfilm, pressing down on the surface of the cheese to exclude as much air as possible. Cover the trays with their lids. **11 .** Leave to cool then label the cheese. Store in a cool, dark place.

Damson Cheese

Damsons are small sour plums. I am often given large trays of them as folk with damson trees tend to despair at how to use up all the fruit from this prolific tree. The main issue, I think, is the ratio of stones to flesh, and so the usual recipes like plum crumble or deep pies don't really work. Damson jam too is hard work, so I usually make jellies or use the fruit to flavour gin.

This year I made some damson cheese. It was quite simple even if sieving the purée took a little longer than in the other cheeses mentioned here.

You can use fresh herbs to flavour the cheese. I like rosemary, which I add by including a couple of big sprigs at the beginning of the cooking process.

Yield **approx. 700g** | *Keeps* **1 year in jars or trays, 1 month in moulds**

1kg damsons
2 large sprigs fresh rosemary
600g white granulated sugar
100ml fresh lemon juice

1 . Begin by washing the damsons well in a colander under cold running water. Chop the rosemary roughly. **2 .** Put the damsons and rosemary into a deep heavy-bottomed pan, and add enough water to just cover the fruit. **3 .** Place the pan over a moderate heat and bring to a simmer. Cover the pan and cook for 15–20 minutes until the damsons are very soft. **4 .** Drain the fruit, discarding the water, then spoon the fruit into a sieve. Using a wooden spoon, rub the purée carefully through the sieve, discarding the stones and skin. Return the purée to the washed pan.

5 . Add the sugar and lemon juice to the damson purée, then cook over a low heat, stirring often, until the sugar has completely dissolved: the mixture should not feel gritty when stirred, and there should be no signs of sugar on the back of your spoon. **6 .** Still keeping the heat low, and stirring often, cook the purée until it is very thick indeed, which can take up to 60 minutes. **7 .** Towards the end of cooking the mixture has a worrying tendency to stick to the bottom of the pan and to coat the sides. Use your wooden spatula to scrape both the sides and the base of the pan frequently, and stir these thicker bits in well. **8 .** When the paste is thick enough to leave a clear channel when you drag the spatula through the bottom of the pan, it is ready to spoon into the moulds. **9 .** Spoon the paste into your chosen flat trays or moulds, and level the tops with a palette knife. **10 .** Put the moulds and trays somewhere cool to set. Cover the moulds with a double layer of clingfilm, pressing it down on to the surface of the cheese to exclude as much air as possible. Cover the trays with their lids. **11 .** Leave to cool then label the cheese. Store in a cool, dark place.

Spiced Crab Apple Cheese

I love the idea of 'free food' and so go scrumping for apples each year when visiting friends in the country. Crab apple trees always seem to fruit prolifically and so whilst I always make some jars of jelly, this recipe, which uses a whole kilogram of crab apples, comes in very useful if I'm over-zealous with my foraging.

I used a silicone cup-cake mould to make small one-serving size cheeses that I wrapped individually in clingfilm and stored in a plastic tub in the fridge.

Yield **approx. 1kg** | *Keeps* **1 year in jars or trays, 1 month in moulds**

1kg crab apples
60g fresh root ginger
500ml water
1 blade of mace
8 allspice berries
6 cloves
1 x 10cm cinnamon stick
500g white granulated sugar

1 . Begin by washing the apples and cutting them into chunks of about 4cm. Finely chop the ginger. **2 .** Place the apples and ginger in a deep heavy-bottomed pan and add the water. **3 .** Place the pan over a moderate heat and bring to a simmer. Cover the pan and cook for 30 minutes until the apples are very soft. You may need to add a little more water. **4 .** Meanwhile finely grind the mace, allspice, cloves and cinnamon, using a spice mill. **5 .** Allow the contents of the pan to cool a little, then spoon into a blender or food processor and whizz until smooth. Rub the purée through a sieve, discarding the fibrous solids that are left. Return the purée to the washed pan. **6 .** Add the sugar and finely ground spices to the pan, then cook over a low heat, stirring often, until the sugar has completely dissolved: the mixture should not feel gritty when stirred, and there should be no signs of sugar on the back of your spoon. **7 .** Still keeping the heat low, and stirring often, cook the purée until it is very thick indeed, when it will become a deep red. This can take up to 2 hours. **8 .** Towards the end of cooking the mixture has a worrying tendency to stick to the bottom of the pan and to coat the sides. Use your wooden spatula to scrape both the sides and the base of the pan frequently, and stir these thicker bits in well. **9 .** When the paste is thick enough to leave a clear channel when you drag the spatula through the bottom of the pan, it is ready to spoon into the moulds. **1 0 .** Spoon the paste into your chosen flat trays or moulds, and level the tops with a palette knife. **1 1 .** Put the moulds and trays somewhere cool to set. Cover the moulds with a double layer of clingfilm, pressing down on to the surface of the cheese to exclude as much air as possible. Cover the trays with their lids. **1 2 .** Leave to cool then label the cheese. Store in a cool, dark place.

Blackcurrant & Apple Cheese

Blackcurrants, especially when mixed with apples, make very good, wonderfully coloured fruit cheese. The pectin in both fruit means that you will have a cheese that is both easy to slice or set in a decorative mould.

I would serve this cheese with toast for breakfast or as part of a buffet table where it would match well with cheese and cold meats.

I used frozen blackcurrants and sharp Bramley apples but you could use any variety.

Yield approx. 1kg | *Keeps* 1 year in jars or trays, 1 month in moulds

1kg blackcurrants
750g Bramley apples
1kg white granulated sugar

1 . Begin by washing the fruit under cold running water to remove any dust. Cut the apples into chunks of about 4cm. **2 .** Place the apples, blackcurrants and water into a deep heavy-bottomed pan, cover and bring to a simmer over a moderate heat. Cook for 20 minutes until everything is very soft, stirring occasionally. **3 .** Allow to cool a little, then spoon the contents of the pan into a blender or food processor and whizz until smooth. Rub the purée through a sieve, discarding the fibrous solids that are left. Return the purée to the washed pan. **4 .** Add the sugar to the fruit then cook over a low heat, stirring often, until the sugar has completely dissolved: the mixture should not feel gritty when stirred, and there should be no signs of sugar on the back of your spoon. **5 .** Still keeping the heat low, and stirring often, cook the purée until it is very thick indeed, when it will become a deep red. This can take anything from 60–90 minutes. **6 .** Towards the end of cooking the mixture has a worrying tendency to stick to the bottom of the pan and to coat the sides. Use your wooden spatula to scrape both the sides and the base of the pan frequently, and stir these thicker bits in well. **7 .** When the paste is thick enough to leave a clear channel when you drag the spatula through the bottom of the pan it is ready to spoon into the moulds. **8 .** Spoon the paste into your chosen flat trays or moulds, and level the tops with a palette knife. **9 .** Put the moulds and trays somewhere cool to set. Cover the moulds with a double layer of clingfilm, pressing it down on to the surface of the cheese to exclude as much air as possible. Cover the trays with their lids. **1 0 .** Leave to cool, then label the cheese. Store in a cool, dark place.

CHUTNEYS

Perfect Chutneys

Why make your own chutney when there are so many good ones now on sale in shops and farmers' markets? Well, apart from my always strongly believing that home-made is best, I love making chutney. It's straightforward, inexpensive and very simple, and in no time at all you have several jars of something delicious that is tailored to your own personal taste.

The word chutney comes from South East Asia, originally 'chatni' in Hindi, and it is mainly from the British Raj that we get our love of these flavoursome preserves. But recipes for such pickles and chutneys can be traced back at least as far as the Middle Ages. There's a wonderful one for garden vegetables steeped in honey and wine, enriched with currants and spiced with ginger and saffron, written on the advent of his marriage by the Goodman of Paris in the last few years of the fourteenth century. Now that's a chutney I'd love to try.

Preserves are common too in references throughout the centuries, from which we learn they would be familiar both to the Romans and to Lord Nelson's Navy where a lime pickle was used to help prevent the scourge that was scurvy on so many of his ships.

Chutneys are wonderfully versatile and can be eaten with any number of varieties of cold meats and cheeses. They spice up the dullest sandwich, and are delicious piled into buttery jacket potatoes.

I love the sweet, sharp, hot flavours that chutney adds to curries and, at my local Indian and Bangladeshi restaurants, I always fight to keep the dishes at the table to eat with the main course rather than just with the appetiser or poppadoms, which is how they are usually served.

A FEW THINGS TO KNOW ABOUT MAKING CHUTNEYS

Simply put, chutneys can be made from a hugely varied mix of ingredients, with spices, chillies and dried fruit added in differing quantities to give you the results you want, but there are one or two guidelines to follow.

★ First you pick your main ingredient, and whether apples, tomatoes, aubergines or plums, you need them to be in good condition. Small bruises can be cut off but good, fresh, ripe fruit and vegetables will always give you the best flavours. Make the chutney with what is most available and seasonal, but beware of trying to use a huge glut of, say, courgettes to make big batches of chutney unless you are sure you have enough friends and family to eat it up.

★ Do try to make the vegetable cubes even in size. This is important, firstly, to ensure they cook at the same rate; and, secondly, so the chutney looks good when served.

★ After the main ingredient come the secondary ones, with onion being ubiquitous. I tend to use either large white or red onions, chopping them into cubes of about 1cm, and making sure no tough brown onion skins gets into the chutney by mistake.

★ Garlic and ginger both feature in many of these recipes, as I love them both. Look for plump, firm garlic and ginger, peeling both and then chopping them finely. Sometimes I make a spice paste by blending these two ingredients with chilli, if I'm using it, and a little vinegar. I do this in a small blender. This has the benefit of making sure these powerful seasoning ingredients will be well distributed in your preserve.

★ Fresh chillies or dried? Well, either work well in chutneys, so the choice is yours. Remember if you use fresh chillies, it is the pith and the seeds than contain the most capsaicin, the 'hot' part of the chilli, so you can regulate the heat by either removing these or leaving them in.

★ Dried fruit is often used to add texture, variety of taste, and to help thicken up the chutney. I think I have used almost every variety of dried fruit in my time, steering clear only of glacé cherries and mixed peel. Ready-to-eat fruits such as apricots and prunes are softer than fully dried ones, and will therefore cook more quickly. Always chop dried fruit, even currants, before you use them.

★ Sugar adds sweetness and helps with the preserving process. I think that for many chutneys, raw, unrefined, light brown sugar works well. If I want the colour of the finished chutney to be bright, I use white granulated sugar. Dark muscovado and molasses sugars are, to my mind, too dominant.

★ Whatever sugar you choose it must be fully dissolved in your preserve before the mixture comes to the boil. Timings involved in dissolving sugar will vary, according to sugar type, heat of liquid etc. You must check that the pan no longer feels gritty, and that there are no signs of sugar crystals on your wooden spoon before continuing with the recipe.

★ Vinegar works with the sugar to provide the preserving and cooking medium. I try and use a suitable vinegar: cider for apple chutneys, or else a simple, tasteless distilled vinegar. I find brown malt vinegar rather a bully of a flavour, but the choice is yours. Here the vinegar can have 5% acidity as the long slow cooking drives off the liquid that would otherwise dilute it.

★ Freshly ground spices really make a difference here. I use my coffee grinder, cleaning it carefully afterwards, but you can use a spice mill. Most spices you have in your store-cupboard can be used in chutney, but be careful not to mix too many to avoid a ragbag flavour.

★ It is of the utmost importance that all vinegar-containing chutneys, relishes and pickles are cooked in a pan that does not react to vinegar. Commonly called 'non-reactive', these pans are

either made from stainless steel or enamelled cast iron.

★ You will need to have jars with vinegar-proof lids for potting chutneys. Either use hinged glass jars with rubber seals or use jam jars that have lids with a rubber seal in them. You can even re-use old jam and pickle jars provided the lids are sound. Cellophane covers are not suitable.

★ As ever cleanliness is very important. All the equipment must be spotlessly clean and the jars will have to be washed, dried, then sterilised for 15–20 minutes in an oven preheated to 100ºC/200ºF/Gas 2.

★ The ingredients for chutneys are usually prepared then cooked together from the start. Beginning over a low heat, the mixture is stirred until the sugar is completely dissolved. I then cover my pan and cook for the next 10 minutes at a low simmer, letting the onions and other ingredients soften.

★ Once the lid is off you can cook over a medium heat until the mixture is thick and rich which could be as long as 40 minutes. Stir the chutney often as you reach this stage since now is when there is the greatest risk of the chutney sticking to the bottom of the pan and thence burning.

★ The test to see if the chutney is cooked enough is simple. Pull a wooden spoon through the mixture. If the two sides remain apart for a few seconds you're ready to pot. If they run together, cook a little longer.

★ Always let the chutney rest for 5 minutes before potting into hot, spotlessly clean jars, packing the chutney down well, to leave no air gaps.

★ Once the jars are cold, you need to check the lids are tightly screwed on, and then you should label the jars clearly, adding the date you made the chutney.

★ Chutneys keep well and improve on storing, being at their best about two to three months after they are made. During this time the flavours can develop and mellow.

★ Store them in a cool, dark place, and try to use them up within a year.

★ As chutneys mature they often darken in colour. This is not a sign they are spoiling.

How to Make the Perfect Jar of Apple & Onion Chutney

This simple apple chutney is a really good place to start. It uses readily available ingredients and shows the basic techniques needed to make any chutney. This is a chutney that I always have handy to add to packed lunch sandwiches.

Yield approx. 1.6 kg | *Keeps* 1 year

Ingredients

1.5kg Bramley or other cooking apples

600g onions

60g garlic

60g fresh root ginger

1–2 fresh red chillies or 1 teaspoon dried chilli flakes (optional)

750ml distilled vinegar

450g light muscovado sugar

2 tablespoons ground turmeric

1 tablespoon fine sea salt

Equipment

Some glass jars with vinegar-proof lids, washed and dried ★ Baking tray ★ Scales and a measuring jug ★ Colander ★ Chopping board and knife ★ Large heavy-bottomed, non-reactive preserving pan with a lid ★ Food processor or liquidiser ★ Spice mill or mortar and pestle ★ Wooden spoon ★ Jam funnel or ladle ★ Labels

1 . Place some clean jars and their lids on a baking tray and then into the oven preheated to 100°C/200°F/Gas 2 for 20 minutes. **2 .** Wash, peel, core and roughly chop the apples. Then put them into your large heavy-bottomed, non-reactive pan. **3 .** Peel and chop the onions more carefully to give a finer dice, about 1cm square, and add these to the apple. **4 .** Peel the garlic and the ginger and chop them and the chillies, if used, into large chunks. Whizz these in a food processor with 100ml of the vinegar to give a paste. Or grind them in a spice mill or in a mortar and pestle. **5 .** Put the garlic and ginger paste and all the remaining ingredients into your pan. **6 .** Place the pan over a low heat. Stir frequently until the soft sugar dissolves, then cover with the lid. **7 .** Bring up to a low simmer and, stirring from time to time, cook the fruit gently for about 10 minutes, or until the onions soften. **8 .** Remove the lid, turn up the heat to medium, and cook the chutney at a moderate boil until thick, about 40 minutes. Stir the pan often, especially towards the end of cooking, as it is then that the chutney will start to stick to the bottom and may burn. **9 .** To test that the chutney is ready, pull a wooden spoon through the centre of the pan. If both sides stay apart you're good to go. If they run together cook a little longer. **10 .** Take the pan from the heat and let it sit for 5 minutes. Take the baking tray of jars from the oven at the same time. **11 .** Pot the chutney into the hot jars, pressing it down well. Be sure to leave a little headspace by filling to the shoulder of the jar and not up the neck. **12** Screw the lids on loosely and leave to cool. **13 .** Once the chutney is cold, check the lids are tight, then label the jars. Store in a cool, dark place.

Bloody Mary Green Beans & Celery Sticks

There is no need to think that drinking Bloody Marys is essential, having made these pickled vegetables, as they would work perfectly in a glass of plain tomato juice. But if you have friends over for brunch, how nice to serve them a Bloody Mary garnished with this unusual pickle.

The beans and celery are pre-cooked in boiling salted water then drained on a clean tea-towel or clean kitchen paper, and patted dry.

I use a potato peeler to remove any strings from the celery as there are few things less elegant than having celery stuck between your front teeth.

Pack the vegetables into a jar deep enough for them to stand up in, and one that has a vinegar-proof lid. I use a 750g jar with a hinged metal top and rubber seal.

Yield approx. 500g | *Keeps* 3 months

200g celery
200g round green beans
2 tablespoons fine sea salt
350ml 6% acidity white wine vinegar
1 teaspoon coriander seeds, crushed
2 bay leaves
1 fresh red chilli, halved
30ml dry sherry
15ml Worcestershire sauce

1 . Start by preparing the vegetables. Peel the strings from the celery, and top and tail the beans. **2 .** Slice the celery into long pieces: they need to be the same length as the beans. **3 .** Blanch the vegetables briefly. Bring a big pan of water to the boil, and add the salt. Have ready a bowl of cold water with some ice cubes in. **4 .** Add the beans to the boiling water, and cook for 3 minutes, adding the celery after 2 minutes. **5 .** Lift the vegetables from the boiling water, using a slotted spoon, and plunge them into the iced water, swishing them about to help them cool quickly. **6 .** Put your chosen jar and its lid into the oven preheated to 100°C/200°F/Gas 2 for 20 minutes. **7 .** Lift the beans and the celery sticks out of the cold water and lay them on a clean, ironed tea-towel or some kitchen paper. Pat them dry. **8 .** Now put the vinegar into a pan with the spices. Put over a low heat, and allow the pan to sit on the heat, without boiling, for 3–4 minutes. **9 .** Bring the jar out of the oven, and rest for 5 minutes. **10 .** Using tongs, pack the vegetables, standing them up as much as you can, into your hot jar. **11 .** Bring the vinegar to the boil, add the sherry and Worcestershire sauce, and pour this into the jar. The vegetables should be completely submerged, by at least 1cm. If not, add more cold vinegar. Scrape all the spices into the jar. **12 .** Screw the vinegar-proof lid on loosely, and leave to cool. **13 .** Once the pickle is cold, check the lid is tight, then label the jar. Store in a cool, dark place. **14 .** The beans and celery are ready for use after a week.

Bread & Butter Pickles

If you are a pickle poker, this might not be the recipe for you, but if like me you enjoy a sweet vinegar tang with your burgers, hot dogs and sandwiches, this cucumber pickle will hit the spot. So called because they are served with sandwiches throughout the USA, bread and butter pickles are simple to make at home, and so very much tastier than shop-bought. They do need to be stored in the fridge, so when choosing your jar size bear this in mind.

Yield **approx. 1.2 kg** | *Keeps* **6 months**

2 large or 4–6 small cucumbers
1 green pepper
1 large mild onion
50g fine sea salt
1 teaspoon black peppercorns
1 teaspoon celery seeds
1 teaspoon fennel seeds
400ml 6% acidity white wine vinegar
200g white granulated sugar
1 teaspoon English mustard powder
1 teaspoon ground turmeric

1 . Cut the cucumbers in half lengthways and, with a small spoon, scrape out and discard the seeds. Now slice the cucumbers finely in whatever shape you choose. **2 .** Halve, seed and finely slice the pepper. Peel and finely slice the onion. **3 .** Put all the prepared vegetables into a glass or plastic bowl large enough to hold them easily. Sprinkle the salt over the vegetables and using your hands toss them together. Cover and leave in a cool place overnight. **4 .** When you are ready to continue, drain the vegetables into a large colander, discarding any liquid that has collected in the bowl, and rinse well under running cold water. **5 .** Spread a clean, ironed tea-towel on the worktop, and lay the vegetables on this, in a single layer, to drain. **6 .** Place some clean jars and their lids on a baking tray and then into the oven preheated to 100°C/200°F/Gas 2 for 20 minutes. **7 .** Crush the whole spices, using either a pestle and mortar or the back of a spoon and a glass bowl, until broken up but not too fine. **8 .** Now pour the vinegar into a large non-reactive pan, and add the sugar and all the spices, including the mustard powder and turmeric. **9 .** Place the pan over a low heat, and stir frequently until the sugar has dissolved: the mixture should not feel gritty when stirred, and there should be no signs of sugar on the back of your spoon. **1 0 .** Bring the mixture to the boil, and simmer for 5 minutes. Remove the baking tray of jars from the oven at the same time. **1 1 .** Add the vegetables to the pan, bring back to the boil and cook for 1 minute only. **1 2 .** Pack the hot vegetables into the hot jars, using tongs and an oven glove, and pressing them down well. You need to leave about 3cm of headspace to allow room for the vinegar to fully cover the vegetables. **1 3 .** Once the vegetables are packed into the jars, pour on the hot pickling liquid, ensuring that the vegetables are completely covered by 1cm. If you are short of liquid top up with a little extra cold vinegar. **1 4 .** Screw the vinegar-proof lids on loosely, and leave to cool. **1 5 .** Once the pickle is cold, check the lids are tight, then label the jars. Store in the fridge. **1 6 .** Leave for at least a week before using.

Giardiniera (Italian Pickled Vegetables)

This is a recipe for those brightly coloured jars of pickled vegetables that you see in Italian delicatessens or pizza parlours. Serve them with cold meats, terrines and pâtés, cheeses, and *antipasto* platters, or take a jar on picnics to enliven your sandwiches.

This recipe comes from my good friend and colleague, Carla Tomasi, with whom I used to teach wonderful wine- and food-filled classes at a cooking school in Italy. We would cook all day and eat, drink and laugh late into the night.

Yield approx. 1kg | *Keeps* 6 weeks

200g each of carrots, cauliflower and small onions or shallots
100g each of red and yellow pepper
200g green string beans
100g celery
100g courgette
650ml 6% acidity white wine vinegar
125ml water
30g white granulated sugar
30g sea salt
2 bay leaves
1 fresh red chilli
1 teaspoon black peppercorns

1 . Begin by preparing the vegetables. Peel and cut the carrots into rings. Break the cauliflower into small florets. Peel the onions and cut into quarters. **2 .** Cut all the pith from the inside of the peppers and remove any seeds. Cut the flesh into strips about 5mm across. **3 .** Top and tail the green beans. Peel the strings from the celery, and then cut the stalks into strips about 5mm across. Cut the courgettes into strips and then dice these. **4 .** Mix the vinegar and water in a large pan, and add the sugar, salt, bay leaves, chilli and peppercorns. **5 .** Place the pan on a low heat and bring to a simmer, stirring until the sugar has dissolved: the mixture should not feel gritty when stirred, and there should be no signs of sugar on the back of your spoon. **6 .** Meanwhile, place some clean jars and their lids on a baking tray and then into the oven preheated to 100°C/200°F/Gas 2 for 20 minutes. **7 .** Put the carrots, onions and cauliflower into the pan of vinegar and water, and cook for 3 minutes. **8 .** Now add the celery, beans and pepper strips, and cook for a further 3 minutes. **9 .** Now put in the courgettes, and cook for a final 2 minutes. Remove the pan from the heat. Take the baking tray of jars from the oven and leave to rest for 5 minutes. **1 0 .** Using a slotted spoon, lift the vegetables from the pickle liquid, and pack them into the hot jars, pressing them down well. You need to leave about 3cm of headspace to allow room for the vinegar to fully cover the vegetables. **1 1 .** Bring the liquid back to boiling point, and cook over a high heat for 2 minutes, then pour this into the jars, ensuring that the vegetables are completely covered by 1cm. If necessary you can add some more cold vinegar. **1 2 .** Screw the vinegar-proof lids on loosely, and leave to cool. **1 3 .** Once the pickle is cold, check the lids are tight, then label the jars. Store in the fridge. **1 4 .** Leave for at least 24 hours before using.

Piccalilli

A recipe for piccalilli is found in a cookbook written by Hannah Glasse in the middle of the eighteenth century. She calls it 'Paco-Lilla' or 'India Pickle', reflecting the heritage that the Empire added to our tables. Pickles and chutneys were commonly found in Indian kitchens and were adopted by Europeans to add relish to the otherwise plain British food.

In this type of pickle, the vegetables are prepared and then brined overnight. Once they have been washed and allowed to dry, they are lightly cooked in a mustard-rich vinegar and sugar sauce. The sauce is thickened using cornflour: it is important that this is fully cooked before you add the vegetables so that no taste of raw flour remains.

Yield **approx. 1.8kg** | *Keeps* **6–9 months**

150g fine sea salt

1.5 litres water

1 small cauliflower

450g small onions or shallots

225g runner beans

2 ridged cucumbers or firm courgettes

1 red pepper

Sauce

2–3 garlic cloves

30g fresh root ginger

1–2 fresh red chillies

1 large cooking apple

750ml 6% acidity distilled vinegar

55g English mustard powder

225g white granulated sugar

1 tablespoon ground turmeric

30g cornflour

1. Make the brine. In a large glass or china bowl dissolve the salt in 500ml boiling water then dilute this with 1 litre of cold water. Put aside to cool. **2.** Now prepare the vegetables. Separate the cauliflower florets, removing any thick stems. Peel the onions and either quarter them or leave whole. You want all the vegetable pieces to be the same size. **3.** Cut the beans into 2cm pieces. Cut the cucumbers in half and scoop out the seeds then dice the flesh. If using courgettes, simply dice them. Discard the seeds and pith of the red pepper and dice the flesh. **4.** Place all the prepared vegetables in the cold brine, cover and leave for 12–18 hours. **5.** The next day drain the vegetables, and wash them thoroughly. **6.** Spread some clean, ironed tea-towels or kitchen paper on the counter and drain the vegetables in a single layer, for about 20 minutes. **7.** Place some clean jars and their lids on a baking tray and then into the oven preheated to 100°C/200°F/Gas 2 for 20 minutes. **8.** Now make the sauce. Peel the garlic and ginger and place in a small food processor or blender. Add the chillies, and whizz together to give a paste. **9.** Peel and grate the apple, discarding the core. **10.** Put the apple and spice paste into a large heavy-bottomed, non-reactive pan, and mix in 250ml of the vinegar. **11.** Place the pan on a low heat, bring to a simmer, cover with the lid, and cook for 5 minutes. **12.** Mix the mustard, sugar, turmeric and cornflour together in a bowl then, using another 250ml vinegar, gradually mix to a smooth paste. Add the remaining vinegar, then scrape this into the pan. **13.** Over a low heat simmer the sauce, stirring constantly, for 3–4 minutes or until you can no longer taste raw cornflour, and the sugar has dissolved. The sauce should be very thick. **14 .** Put the vegetables into the pan and stir well. The sauce may not completely cover them, but mix them around in it. Cook over a gentle heat, stirring often, until the vegetables just soften slightly, about 10 minutes. The sauce may thin a little as some of the juice from the vegetables comes out. **15 .** Meanwhile, take the baking tray of jars from the oven, and leave for 5 minutes.

16 . Spoon the piccalilli into the hot jars, pressing it down well. Make sure the vegetables are covered by the sauce by at least 1cm. Add more cold vinegar if needed. **17 .** Screw on the lids loosely, and leave to cool. **18 .** Once the pickle is cold, check the lids are tight, then label the jars. Store in a cool, dark place. **19 .** Leave for at least a week before eating, but it will be better if you can wait a month.

Pickled Beetroot

Pickled beetroot is simple to make, and so that may be why it's said to be the most common home-made pickle. But another reason is that beetroots need constant thinning when growing, so jars of this pickle can be made throughout the summer.

I prefer to use small beets, but if you have mixed sizes, cut them, once cooked, into pieces roughly the same size. These days you can find beets of many differing colours. If you want to show this, don't mix the colours in your jars, the red ones will bleed into the vinegar, colouring all the rest.

When you come to peel the beets do please wear gloves or the beets will stain your hands quite dramatically.

Yield **approx. 1.2kg** | *Keeps* **up to 6 months**

1kg raw beetroot, trimmed weight
500ml 6% acidity distilled vinegar
100g white granulated sugar
1 blade of mace
1 x 10cm cinnamon stick
2 fresh bay leaves
½ teaspoon each of black peppercorns and
  allspice berries
1 dried red chilli
finely grated zest of 1 orange

1 . Begin by washing off all the soil from the beetroots. **2 .** Place the prepared beets into a large pan and cover them with cold water. Bring them to the boil, then turn the heat down until the pot is held at a simmer. **3 .** Cook for between 15 and 30 minutes. If the beets are of differing sizes, you will need to remove the small beets once they can be pierced through with a sharp skewer, leaving the larger ones until they are cooked through. **4 .** Drain the beets and allow them to cool. **5 .** Meanwhile pour the vinegar into another pan, add the sugar, spices and orange zest, bring up to boiling point and turn off the heat. Stir well to ensure the sugar is dissolved. **6 .** Place some clean jars and their lids on a baking tray and then into the oven preheated to 100°C/200°F/Gas 2 for 20 minutes. **7 .** Once the beets are cool enough to handle, slip off their skins and cut them into even-sized pieces. **8 .** Remove the baking tray of jars from the oven and leave to rest for 5 minutes. **9 .** Pack the beet dice into the hot jars, pressing them down well. You need to leave about 3cm of headspace to allow room for the vinegar to fully cover the beetroot. **10 .** Now bring the vinegar back to boiling point, then pour this into the jars, ensuring that the onions are completely covered by 1cm. Add more vinegar, which can be cold, straight from the bottle, if required. Divide the spices between the jars. **11 .** Screw the vinegar-proof lids on loosely, and leave to cool. **12 .** Once the pickle is cold, check the lids are tight, then label the jars. Store in a cool, dark place. **13 .** Leave for at least a week before using.

Pickled Runner Beans

Single vegetable pickles are not that unusual. We don't turn a hair at the thought of pickled onions or beetroot, yet runner beans, one of my favourite and very seasonal vegetables, usually end up playing a bit part in that catch-all pickle, piccalilli. It is time to change all this. Pickled runner beans are delicious, more especially if you can pick relatively young beans from your garden before they become tough and stringy. I like to serve them with bread and cheese.

I cook the beans lightly before covering with the pickle as I find that gives the best result – the beans are still crunchy but not raw. After you have cooked and refreshed the beans spread them on a clean tea-towel and pat them dry. I iron my tea-towels not for smartness, but because a hot iron kills any bacteria on them.

Don't skimp on the salt here. Most of it will be thrown away when you drain the beans, and they need the seasoning a tablespoon gives. If you prefer sweeter pickles, an extra spoonful or two of sugar can be added.

Yield **approx. 550g** | *Keeps* **up to 6 months**

300g freshly picked runner beans
1 tablespoon fine sea salt
350ml 6% acidity white wine or distilled vinegar
¼ teaspoon celery seeds
1 blade of mace
1 tablespoon white granulated sugar

1 . Start by preparing the beans. Top and tail them, removing any side strings. **2 .** Cut the beans into 5cm pieces. I do this on a slant to make them look a little more professional. **3 .** Blanch the beans. Bring a big pan of water to the boil, and add the salt. Have a bowl of iced water ready. **4 .** Add the beans to the salted water, return to the boil and cook for 3 minutes. **5 .** Drain the beans and plunge them into the iced water, swishing them around so they cool quickly. Drain the beans and lay them on a clean, ironed tea-towel to dry. **6 .** Place some clean jars and their lids on a baking tray and then into the oven preheated to 100°C/200°F/Gas 2 for 20 minutes. **7 .** Put the vinegar, spices and sugar into a small saucepan and place this over a low heat, stirring to dissolve the sugar: the mixture should not feel gritty when stirred, and there should be no signs of sugar on the back of your spoon. **8 .** Allow the vinegar to sit, not boiling but gently simmering, over the heat for 3–4 minutes. Remove the baking tray of jars from the oven and leave to rest for 5 minutes. **9 .** Pat the beans dry with absorbent kitchen paper then, using tongs, pack them into the hot jars, pressing them down well. Leave about 3cm of headspace to allow room for the vinegar to fully cover the fruit/veg. **10 .** Bring the vinegar to the boil and pour into the jars, ensuring that the beans are completely covered by 1cm. Add some more cold vinegar if needed. Divide any remaining spices between the jars. **11 .** Screw the vinegar-proof lids on loosely, and leave to cool. **12 .** Once the pickle is cold, check the lids are tight, then label the jars. Store in a cool, dark place. **13 .** Leave for a week before using.

Ploughman's Pickle

This brown pickle is rich and fragrant. The sauce is thickened with both cornflour and apple. It takes a bit of time to prepare, as the vegetables must be chopped into even 1cm dice so the finished pickle cooks properly and tastes as it should.

Yield approx. 2.8 kg | *Keeps* up to 6 months

400g cauliflower

300g firm small courgettes

250g small turnips

250g tender young carrots

100g onions

1 celery heart

3 tablespoons fine sea salt

450g Bramley or other soft-cooking apples

30g garlic

1 litre 6% acidity malt vinegar

55g cornflour

500g dark muscovado sugar

1 teaspoon each of ground cinnamon and turmeric

1 teaspoon each of ground nutmeg and allspice

1/4 teaspoon cayenne pepper (optional)

1 . Begin by preparing the vegetables. Cut the cauliflower into tiny florets. Slice the courgettes into batons and dice these. Peel and dice the turnips, carrots and onion. Dice the celery heart. **2 .** Then blanch the vegetables. Bring a big pan of water to the boil and put in the salt. Have a bowl of iced water ready nearby. **3 .** One vegetable at a time, blanch the vegetables: the turnips and carrots need 3 minutes, the cauliflower, celery and onion, 2 minutes, and the courgettes only 30 seconds. **4 .** As each batch is ready remove them from the pan with a slotted spoon. Pass them through the iced water, then remove with the slotted spoon and lay them on clean, ironed tea-towels or absorbent kitchen paper to dry. **5 .** Peel, core and dice the apples. Peel and crush the garlic. **6 .** Place the apple and garlic in a large saucepan with about 250ml of the vinegar, cover the pan and cook until the apple is soft, about 20 minutes. **7 .** Place some clean jars and their lids on a baking tray and then into the oven preheated to 100°C/200°F/Gas 2 for 20 minutes. **8 .** Mix the cornflour with 4 tablespoons of the remaining vinegar and set aside. **9 .** Pour the rest of the vinegar, the sugar and spices into the apple/garlic mixture and stir over a low heat until the sugar has dissolved. **10 .** Mix a few spoonfuls of the hot vinegar sauce into the cornflour and then scrape all this into the pan. Using a whisk, cook the sauce until thick and smooth, about 3 minutes. Taste to check no trace of raw cornflour remains. **11 .** Give the vegetables a final pat dry with kitchen paper, and then tip them into the pan. Stir them carefully with a spoon making sure they are all coated with the sauce. **12 .** Cook for 5 minutes, remove the baking tray from the oven and leave the jars to rest for 5 minutes. **13 .** Pot the vegetables into the hot jars, pressing them down well. Spoon over the sauce, ensuring it covers the vegetables by 1cm. Add more cold vinegar if needed. **14 .** Screw on the vinegar-proof lids loosely, and leave to cool. **15 .** When the pickle is cold, check the lids are tight, then label the jars. Store in a cool, dark place. **16 .** Whilst this pickle can be used within the week, it is better if left for a month to mature.

Spiced Pickled Peaches

Peaches, so wonderful and fragrant, are plentiful in summer and can be preserved in many ways. I poach them lightly in sugar syrup then peel and store them in jars of brandy, or I make jam and jellies, but I think I love this savoury way of pickling them best of all. Delicious with cold meats at a summer picnic, these spiced peaches will add a touch of sunshine to a dark winter's day too.

Choose small, firm peaches or, if you'd rather not go to the bother of peeling them, you can just as easily choose nectarines. I roast the fruit first to both soften it and concentrate the flavours.

Yield **approx. 1kg** | *Keeps* **9 months**

750g firm peaches
300g caster sugar
400ml 6% acidity white wine vinegar
1 x 10cm cinnamon stick
4 cardamom pods
1 fresh red chilli, quartered
a strip of orange zest

1 . Preheat the oven to 200°C/400°F/Gas 6.
2 . Peel the peaches first. Cut a small cross in the base of each peach and then place them in a bowl. Now cover the fruit with boiling water and leave for 60 seconds. Lift them from the bowl one at a time, using a slotted spoon, and remove the peel. **3 .** Now quarter the peaches and discard the stones. Place the peach flesh on a baking sheet lined with non-stick paper. Sprinkle about 50g of the measured sugar over them, and roast in the preheated oven for 30 minutes. **4 .** Meanwhile, prepare the spiced vinegar. Mix the remaining sugar with the vinegar in a stainless-steel saucepan.
5 . Crush the cinnamon and cardamom a little with a rolling pin, and add to the vinegar. **6 .** Place the pan over a low heat, and stir frequently until the sugar has dissolved: the mixture should not feel gritty when stirred, and there should be no signs of sugar crystals on the back of your spoon. **7 .** Bring the vinegar to a boil and simmer for 5 minutes. Turn off and allow the flavours to infuse until needed.
8 . Remove the peaches from the oven, and turn the oven temperature down to 100°C/200°F/Gas 2.
9 . Place some glass jars and their lids on a baking tray and into the cooler oven for 20 minutes. When ready, take the jars from the oven and leave to rest for 5 minutes. **10 .** Now, using tongs and an oven glove, lift the peaches from the tray and put them into the hot jars, pressing them down so they are well packed in. You need to leave about 3cm of headspace to allow room for the vinegar to fully cover the fruit. **11 .** Bring the vinegar up to boiling point, then pour this into the jars, ensuring that the peaches are completely covered by 1cm. Add more vinegar, which can be cold, straight from the bottle, if required. Tuck the spices and chilli into the jars. **12 .** Screw the vinegar-proof lids on loosely, and leave to cool. **13 .** Once the pickle is cold, check the lids are tight, then label the jars. Store in a cool, dark place. **14 .** Leave for at least a month before using.

Pickled Rhubarb

I first tasted this pretty pink pickle at my local pub, the lovely Drapers Arms in Barnsbury, Islington. The chef, James de Jong, makes wonderful things with pork: Scotch eggs, sausage rolls, pies, *rillettes* and the like. With them he serves home-made pickles and in spring, when the rhubarb comes down from the Rhubarb Triangle in Yorkshire, and is tender and beautifully pink, he makes this.

Rhubarb tends to have a lot of juice, and breaks down to a pulp when cooked, so Chef de Jong uses it raw, covered with the hot pickle mixture and stored in a cold store-room or the fridge, where it will keep for up to three months. Once you have used the rhubarb, you can use the vinegar in salad dressings and sauces.

Choose thin stems of very fresh rhubarb and wipe them clean with damp kitchen paper rather than washing them.

Yield approx. 550g | *Keeps* 3 months

500g forced rhubarb

300ml 6% acidity white wine vinegar

150g white granulated sugar

1 star anise

1 cinnamon stick

1 clove

1 teaspoon coriander seeds

1 teaspoon fennel seeds

½ teaspoon ground white pepper

1 fresh red chilli

2 bay leaves

1 . Wipe any dust and dirt from the stems of rhubarb and cut them diagonally into 5cm pieces. **2 .** Put one large or two smaller clean glass jars and their lids on to a baking tray and into the oven preheated to 100°C/200°F/Gas 2 for 20 minutes. **3 .** Pour the vinegar into a saucepan and add the sugar, the spices and the aromatics. **4 .** Put the pan over a low heat and heat until the sugar fully dissolves: the mixture should not feel gritty when stirred, and there should be no signs of sugar on the back of your spoon. **5 .** Turn off the heat and allow the flavours to infuse for 10 minutes. **6 .** Take the baking tray of jars from the oven and allow to rest for 5 minutes. **7 .** Pack the cold rhubarb pieces carefully into the hot jars, using a spoon, and pressing it down well. You need to leave about 3cm of headspace to allow room for the vinegar to fully cover the rhubarb. **8 .** Bring the vinegar up to boiling point, and pour into the jars, ensuring that the rhubarb is completely covered by 1cm. You may need to add a little more cold vinegar. **9 .** Screw the vinegar-proof lids on loosely, and leave to cool. **1 0 .** Once the pickle is cold, check the lids are tight, then label the jars. You may need to press the rhubarb down under the vinegar again. Store in the fridge. **1 1 .** This is best left for a week before using.

Kimchi

This Korean pickle is gaining in popularity and as it's quite simple to make at home, I've included a recipe here. It is served alongside almost every dish I've eaten in Korean restaurants, and adds a sour, strong and tangy flavour to food. *Kimchi* is also said to be good for the digestion and all-round health. The first taste is not for the faint-hearted, but it's one of those slow burn pickles: after a while you'll just keep reaching for the jar.

Kimchi is made by *lacto-fermentation*, not by pickling in vinegar, and in this it resembles *sauerkraut*. The brined vegetables ferment, with *Lactobacillus*, a friendly bacterium, converting sugars in the vegetables into acids. These give a bright, slightly fizzy flavour to this fiery pickle.

I used Chinese leaf and radish for my *Kimchi*: there are as many recipes as there are Korean families, but this seems fairly standard. Use red radish or mouli, either is fine. Be sure to use sea salt for the brine, as the anti-caking agent in some table salts tends to stop fermentation.

Store your *Kimchi* in a spotlessly clean glass jar: I used one with a hinged glass lid and rubber washer. Wash, dry and sterilise in a low oven – preheated to 100ºC/200ºF/Gas 2 – in the usual way.

My pantry is cold enough to store it in winter, but in summer keep it in the fridge.

Yield approx. 1kg | *Keeps* 4-6 weeks

1 large head Chinese leaf
200g radish, trimmed weight
40g fine sea salt
1–2 litres water
6 spring onions
60g fresh root ginger
40g garlic
50ml Thai fish sauce
30g gochugaru (Korean chilli flakes)
15g white granulated sugar

1 . Begin by slicing the Chinese leaf into biggish chunks about 5cm square. Slice the radishes into discs. **2 .** Place the vegetables in a large glass or china bowl. Sprinkle on the salt and rub this well into the vegetables. **3 .** Add 1–2 litres of water so the vegetables are covered in the brine and leave for 4 hours. **4 .** Cut the spring onions into 5cm lengths, and keep to one side. **5 .** Peel the ginger and garlic, and whizz them in a blender or processor until a paste is formed. Or chop them very finely. **6 .** In a small bowl mix the garlic/ginger paste with the fish sauce, gochugaru and sugar. **7 .** Drain the cabbage and radish from the brine, keeping some of the brine, and return them to the large bowl. **8 .** Add the spring onions to the bowl as well, then scrape in your seasoning mix. **9 .** Wearing plastic or rubber gloves, knead the mix into the vegetables until thoroughly coated. **10 .** Pack the mixture into your large clean glass jar, pressing it down well. You want to add a little of the juices/brine, enough to cover the solids by 1cm. Cover loosely with a vinegar-proof lid. **11 .** Let the jar stand at room temperature for 1–5 days, pressing down on the vegetables each day, using a clean metal spoon. You want to keep them submerged under the brine. When you open the lid you may notice a slight fizz as the air escapes; this means the *kimchi* is fermenting well. **12 .** Taste the *kimchi*, and when it is strong enough for you, move the jar to a cold place.

RELISHES

Perfect Relishes

Relish. The name says it all. When you open this jar, you know you will be adding savour to your food. Your taste-buds will be excited, and an otherwise perhaps rather dull dish will sparkle with the zing a relish gives to it.

But what is the difference between a relish, a chutney and a pickle? Semantics apart, I feel that a pickle is a preserve where the chosen vegetable is brined and then submerged in flavoured vinegar and left to develop; a chutney is one where the vegetables and fruit are slow-cooked with sugar, vinegar and spices until thick and deep in flavour, and it too is usually left to mellow; whereas a relish is quick cooked, can be eaten at once, and has a lighter fresher flavour and crunch.

Relishes are the perfect accompaniment for barbecues; they should be packed into picnic baskets, decanted into small pots and popped into lunch-boxes, and they should grace the table at high tea. Whenever you need to add a little extra oomph to your food, serving a relish is definitely the way to go.

A FEW THINGS TO KNOW ABOUT MAKING RELISHES

★ A relish usually has both sweet, sour and hot notes in it, combining fruits and vegetables, sugar and vinegar and fresh herbs, with sometimes more than a touch of chilli.

★ As relishes are usually only lightly cooked, they do not have the keeping qualities of more preserved pickles. As a result, they should be made in small batches and stored in the refrigerator. They often haven't enough sugar or vinegar to be stored on the pantry shelf.

★ I use light-tasting vinegars for relishes: white wine, cider and distilled vinegars work well. Malt vinegar and light-tasting but low-acidity rice wine vinegars are not usually the best choice.

★ Again I tend to use a sugar that is light in flavour to let the fresh taste of the vegetables be the star in these relishes. If you prefer you could use a raw, lightly coloured, soft brown sugar. Whichever sugar you choose it must be fully dissolved in your preserve before continuing with the recipe. Timings involved in dissolving sugar will vary, according to sugar type, heat of liquid etc. You must check that the pan no longer feels gritty, and that there are no signs of sugar crystals on your wooden spoon.

★ Freshly ground whole spices add flavour and zing here as elsewhere. I like to keep the flavours simple, but you can experiment with tastes you like, making the recipe your own.

★ Choose the freshest fruit and vegetables for relishes, as their charm lies in the quality of the ingredients. While I've given my favourites, there is no reason why, if you have some sweet young carrots, say, you couldn't use the recipe for radish relish to make a carrot relish, adding some crushed coriander seeds, perhaps.

★ I find fresh chillies work best in relishes. Take care when using them, as the oil will remain on your fingers for some time. You can regulate the heat in the relish by either taking the seeds and pith out of the chillies before you chop them or leaving them in.

★ When you make a relish it is important that you chop the vegetables evenly. A small even dice will make the finished relish more palatable; it will look more tempting and the pieces will cook evenly.

★ The methods for making the different relishes vary somewhat, and you will notice that some are thickened with cornflour. If the recipe uses this, you simply mix the given quantity with either a little water or some of the liquid from the relish itself, and then stir this into the relish while it cooks. Cornflour needs about 3–4 minutes' cooking to make sure there is no taste of raw flour lingering in your preserve.

★ As all relishes contain vinegar you will need to use a non-reactive, acid-resistant pan when you are cooking them.

★ The jars in which you store your relishes must have lids with vinegar-proof seals. Cellophane covers are not suitable here.

★ And, as usual, the jars and their lids must be spotlessly clean, having been washed, dried, and sterilised in the oven preheated to 100ºC/200ºF/ Gas 2 for 20 minutes.

★ Most relishes should be kept in the fridge for no longer than four to six weeks.

How to Make the Perfect Jar of Tomato Relish

I love this relish and make it often. It uses things I normally have in my fridge and store-cupboard, and is delicious piled on to hamburgers or hot dogs. Crushed fennel adds a delicious aniseed flavour, but crushed coriander or cumin seeds would work too.

Yield approx. 600g | *Keeps* 6 weeks

Ingredients

1 large red onion

2 plump garlic cloves

60ml olive oil

500g ripe tomatoes

1 fresh red chilli

1 teaspoon fennel seeds

75g light muscovado sugar

90ml red or white wine vinegar

1 teaspoon fine sea salt

½ teaspoon ground black pepper

2–3 tablespoons fresh coriander, tarragon or basil leaves, chopped

Equipment

Scales and a measuring jug ★ Some glass jars and vinegar-proof lids, washed and dried ★ Baking tray ★ Chopping board and sharp knife ★ Large heavy-bottomed, non-reactive preserving pan with a lid ★ Pestle and mortar ★ Wooden spoon ★ Large metal spoon ★ Labels

1. Place some clean jars and their lids on a baking tray and then into the oven preheated to 100°C/200°F/Gas 2 for 20 minutes. **2.** Begin by preparing the vegetables. Peel and chop the onions into 5mm dice, and then peel and chop the garlic cloves finely. **3.** Heat the oil in a large heavy-bottomed pan and cook the onion and garlic over a low to medium heat until soft, about 15 minutes. **4.** While the onions and garlic soften, prepare the tomatoes. I leave the skins on large tomatoes for a chunky relish, but if you have a real aversion to tomato skin, do peel them (see the Glossary, page 20). **5.** Cut the tomatoes into 1cm dice, removing and discarding the stringy core, and add the flesh to the pan with the onions. **6.** Finely chop the chilli. Crush the fennel seeds lightly and add these to the pan along with the sugar, vinegar, salt and pepper. **7.** Place the pan over a low heat, and simmer, stirring with a wooden spoon, until the sugar has dissolved. **8.** Now turn up the heat and simmer the relish for 5–7 minutes until most of the liquid has been driven off and the mixture is thick. **9.** Remove the baking tray of jars from the oven and let the jars rest for 5 minutes. **10.** Take the pan from the heat and stir in the chopped herbs. **11.** Spoon the relish into the hot jars, using a metal spoon, and pressing down well. The relish should reach a little up the shoulder of the jar, leaving most of the neck as headspace. **12.** Put the lids on loosely and leave to cool. **13.** Once the relish is cold, check the lids are tight, then label the jars. Store in the fridge.

Cucumber Relish

This relish reminds me of my three years living in North America, where the certainty of summer sunshine meant picnics and barbecues aplenty. Tall jars of relish were always served arranged on a side table with squirty mustard, paper plates, napkins and ghastly plastic cups of non-alcoholic Tropical Punch. Tomato, sweetcorn, and cucumber were favourites, so I'm including all these in this chapter.

Yield **approx. 1.2kg** | *Keeps* **6 weeks**

2 large English-style cucumbers
1 teaspoon fine sea salt
100g celery
100g onion
1 fresh green chilli
½ teaspoon mustard seeds
½ teaspoon celery seeds
200ml 6% acidity white wine vinegar
75g white granulated sugar
1 teaspoon cornflour
1 tablespoon water

1 . Place some clean jars and their lids on a baking tray and then into the oven preheated to 100°C/200°F/Gas 2 for 20 minutes. **2 .** Start by preparing your vegetables. Split the cucumbers lengthways and scoop out the seeds. Discard these. Now slice the cucumber into strips and cut into tiny dice of about 5mm. **3 .** Place the cucumber cubes in a colander and sprinkle on the salt evenly. Leave this to drip while you prepare the remaining vegetables. **4 .** Using a potato peeler peel the outer side of the celery to remove the strings. Peel the onion. Chop the celery and onion into tiny dice the same size as the cucumber cubes. **5 .** Chop the chilli very finely. Crush the mustard and celery seeds, using a mortar and pestle. **6 .** Place the celery, onion, chilli and crushed seeds, along with the vinegar, into a shallow, heavy-bottomed, non-reactive pan. **7 .** Place the pan over a low heat, cover with the lid, and simmer for 5 minutes to soften the vegetables. **8 .** Wash the cucumber under a running cold tap, then spread the cubes on a clean, ironed tea-towel and pat dry. **9 .** Tip these into the pan, add the sugar, and cook over a low heat until the sugar has dissolved: the mixture should not feel gritty when stirred, and there should be no signs of sugar on the back of your spoon. **10 .** Now bring to the boil and cook at a high boil for 2 minutes. **11 .** Mix the cornflour and water together, and stir this into the pan. Cook at a simmer for a further 3–4 minutes, stirring constantly, or until the sauce has thickened slightly and no taste of the cornflour remains. **12 .** Remove the baking tray of jars from the oven, and leave to rest for 5 minutes. **13 .** Pot the relish into the hot jars, using a metal spoon, and pressing down well. The relish should reach a little up the shoulder of the jar, leaving most of the neck as headspace. **14 .** Put the lids on loosely and leave to cool. **15 .** Once the relish is cold, check the lids are tight, then label the jars. Store in a cool, dark place, ideally the fridge.

Sweetcorn Relish

This lovely relish is easily made with frozen corn, but if you can buy very fresh corn from a market or, better yet, if you grow it in your garden, then that is best of all.

Corn should be cooked as soon after it is picked as possible, as the sugars in the corn begin turning to starch once the cobs are separated from the plant. Never add salt to water when you're cooking corn, which makes it tough. Always season at the end of the cooking.

The vegetables in a relish should always be the same size. In a corn relish, the size of the kernels dictates the size of the chop.

Yield **approx. 900g** | *Keeps* **4–6 weeks**

400g sweetcorn kernels
125g red onion
125g celery
75g sweet red pepper
1–2 large hot, fresh red chillies
30g garlic
1 teaspoon fennel seeds
200ml 6% acidity white wine vinegar
100g white granulated sugar
10g cornflour
1 teaspoon fine sea salt
½ teaspoon finely ground black pepper

1 . Place some clean jars and their lids on a baking tray and then into the oven preheated to 100°C/200°F/Gas 2 for 20 minutes. **2 .** Begin by preparing the vegetables. If using frozen corn allow it to thaw. Blanch the corn in a pan of boiling water for 3 minutes. **3 .** Peel and finely dice the onion. Run a potato peeler down the outside of the celery sticks to remove strings. Cut the flesh into fine strips then cut these into tiny dice too. **4 .** Remove the pith and seeds from the red pepper, and cut the flesh into tiny dice. Chop the chillies into tiny dice. **5 .** Peel and crush the garlic. Crush the fennel seeds. **6 .** Put all the prepared vegetables and flavourings into a deep, heavy-bottomed, non-reactive pan and add the vinegar and sugar. **7 .** Place the pan over a low heat, and simmer, stirring, until the sugar has dissolved: the mixture should not feel gritty when stirred, and there should be no signs of sugar on the back of your spoon. **8 .** Cover with the lid, and simmer the relish for 10 minutes. **9 .** Take the lid from the pan and turn up the heat. Simmer for 5 minutes, until most of the liquid has gone. **10 .** Now mix the cornflour with a couple of tablespoons of water, and stir this into the relish. Cook over a low heat for 3–4 minutes, or until the sauce has thickened slightly and no taste of uncooked cornflour remains. Stir in the salt and pepper. **11 .** Meanwhile, remove the baking tray of jars from the oven, and leave to rest for 5 minutes. **12 .** Pot the relish into the hot jars, using a metal spoon, and pressing down well. The relish should reach a little up the shoulder of the jar, leaving most of the neck as headspace. **13 .** Screw the lids on loosely and leave to cool. **14 .** Once the relish is cold, check the lids are tight, then label the jars. Store in a cool, dark place, ideally the fridge.

Summer Vegetable Relish

This lovely relish sits between fresh relishes and chutneys, as it uses vegetables that need a little more cooking than some, but still keeps its clean fresh flavour. It is a little like a ratatouille, and uses all those summer vegetables that arrive with a rush and can, if you grow them at home, result in a glut.

I love serving this with barbecued lamb, but it works well with any Mediterranean-style food. When you serve it, fold in some fresh chopped mint, basil, thyme or dill to accent the dishes.

As I'm cooking this for longer than a usual relish, I'm using a vinegar with only 5% acidity. The higher sugar content also helps as a preservative.

Choose small ripe tomatoes and skin them before you cook them. Small firm courgettes and firm aubergines are best too.

Yield **approx. 1.5kg** | *Keeps* **3 months**

450g tomatoes
300g aubergine
200g red peppers
400g courgette
200g red onion
2 fresh hot red chillies, or to taste
4 plump garlic cloves
1 tablespoon fine sea salt
1 tablespoon fennel seeds
1 tablespoon coriander seeds
2 tablespoons dried oregano
300g white granulated sugar
500ml 5% acidity cider vinegar

1. Start by preparing all the vegetables. Skin the tomatoes (see the Glossary, page 20), then chop them, cutting away any hard cores. **2.** Chop the aubergine, cutting the flesh into 1cm dice. **3.** Cut the peppers in half, removing the stems. Scrape out and discard all the seeds and pith, then cut the flesh into 1cm cubes as well. Dice the courgette. **4.** Peel and chop the onion. Chop the chillies finely, and peel and crush the garlic. **5.** Mix the salt, seeds and oregano in a pestle, and crush together with a mortar. **6.** Now place all the ingredients in a large heavy-bottomed, non-reactive pan. **7.** Place this over a moderate heat and, stirring often, bring the mixture slowly to the boil. Make sure the sugar has completely dissolved: the mixture should not feel gritty when stirred, and there should be no signs of sugar on the back of your spoon. **8.** Simmer, uncovered, until thick, about 45 minutes. Take care towards the end of cooking time that you stir the bottom of the pan well, as the relish has a dreadful tendency to stick and burn. **9.** Meanwhile, place some clean jars and their lids on a baking tray and then into the oven preheated to 100°C/200°F/Gas 2 for 20 minutes. When ready to pot, remove from the oven and leave to rest for 5 minutes. **10.** Pot the relish into the hot jars, using a metal spoon, and pressing down well. The relish should reach a little up the shoulder of the jar, leaving most of the neck as headspace. **11.** Screw the lids on loosely and leave to cool. **12.** Once the relish is cold, check the lids are tight, then label the jars. Store in a cool, dark place.

Blueberry Relish

Blueberries make a vibrant relish full of fruit flavours, and vivid enough to brighten the dullest plate of food. They are at their most available in late summer when British bushes fruit, and it is then that I'd choose to make this relish.

I've used coriander in the spice mix, as the flavour of this spice is meant to enhance the blueberries. If you can pick fresh coriander seeds from a plant that has flowered, use these: they have the wonderful crossover flavour of both the dried seed and the green herb.

Yield **approx. 600g** | *Keeps* **up to 6 weeks**

300g fresh blueberries
200g celery
200g onion
1 fresh red chilli, or to taste
150ml 6% acidity white wine vinegar
1 x 10cm cinnamon stick
2 teaspoons coriander seeds
1 teaspoon fresh thyme leaves
100g white granulated sugar
½ teaspoon cornflour
1 tablespoon water

1 . Place some clean jars and their lids on a baking tray and then into the oven preheated to 100°C/200°F/Gas 2 for 20 minutes. **2 .** Start by preparing the fruit and vegetables. If the blueberries look dusty, give them a brief wash under a cold tap. De-string the celery, using a potato peeler, and peel the onion. **3 .** Chop the celery and onion into small even dice. Chop the chilli finely. **4 .** Put the vegetables, blueberries and flavourings into a wide, heavy-bottomed, non-reactive pan, and add the vinegar and the cinnamon stick. **5 .** Cover the pan, put it on a low heat and cook the blueberries until they pop and are tender, about 5 minutes. The celery and onion will still be crunchy. **6 .** Crush the coriander seeds and thyme leaves together in a mortar and pestle, and tip into the pan along with the sugar. Stir until the sugar dissolves: the mixture should not feel gritty when stirred, and there should be no signs of sugar on the back of your spoon. **7 .** Mix the cornflour and water together, and stir this into the relish. Now simmer for a further 4–5 minutes, stirring constantly. The sauce will thicken slightly. You must make sure the flour is cooked through and that no taste of raw flour remains. **8 .** Take the pan from the heat, discard the cinnamon stick and let the relish stand for 2 minutes. Remove the baking tray of jars from the oven at the same time and leave to rest for 5 minutes. **9 .** Pot the relish into the hot jars, using a metal spoon, and pressing down well. The relish should reach a little up the shoulder of the jar, leaving most of the neck as headspace. **1 0 .** Screw the lids on loosely and leave to cool. **1 1 .** Once the relish is cold, check the lids are tight, then label the jars. Store in a cool, dark place, ideally the fridge.

Pineapple Relish

This aromatic relish comes from the West Indies, via a good friend of mine, Catherine Phipps. She cooked there for a while, and came back with a wealth of great recipes and ideas.

Choose a ripe pineapple: pick one that is heavy in your hand and hold it up by one of the leaves. If the pineapple drops, the leaf coming off in your hand, the fruit is ripe. You will probably need to buy a pineapple that weighs about 1kg to give you the 500g needed in this recipe.

Yield **approx. 600g** | *Keeps* **3 months**

500g fresh pineapple, prepared weight
200g red onion
1 fresh red chilli
45g fresh root ginger
100g raw, soft light brown sugar
100ml 6% acidity cider vinegar
½ teaspoon fine sea salt
zest and juice of 1 lime

Spice bouquet garni
1 bay leaf
1 teaspoon allspice berries
1 x 2.5cm cinnamon stick
1 teaspoon coriander seeds
1 teaspoon black peppercorns
½ blade of mace
2 cloves
2 cardamom pods

1 . Begin by preparing the pineapple. Cut away all the rough skin and eyes from the pineapple then cut lengthways into quarters and cut away the core. Cut the pineapple quarters in half lengthways again then thinly slice the pineapple across to give small pieces. **2 .** Peel the onion and finely chop. Finely chop the chilli. Peel and finely grate the ginger. I use the side of a teaspoon to peel the ginger, and the fine holes of a grater to grate it. **3 .** Make the the bouquet garni. Put all the ingredients into a scalded piece of muslin or cheesecloth and tie firmly. Bash around a little with a mallet or rolling pin, just to help the flavours on their way. **4 .** Put the sugar, vinegar, salt, ginger, chilli and the bouquet garni into a large non-reactive, heavy-bottomed saucepan. **5 .** Place the pan over a low heat and cook gently, stirring, until the sugar has dissolved. **6 .** Now bring the mixture up to boiling point and add the remaining ingredients, the pineapple, onion, lime juice and zest. Reduce to a simmer, and stirring often, cook until the mixture has thickened a little, about 30–45 minutes. The pineapple will still hold its shape. **7 .** Meanwhile, place some clean jars and their lids on a baking tray and then into the oven preheated to 100°C/200°F/Gas 2 for 20 minutes, then remove from the oven and rest for 5 minutes. **8 .** Discard the spice package, then spoon the relish into the hot jars, pressing down well. The relish should reach a little up the shoulder of the jar, leaving most of the neck as headspace. **9 .** Screw the lids on loosely and leave to cool. **1 0 .** Once the relish is cold, check the lids are tight, then label the jars. Store in a cool, dark place, ideally the fridge.

Radish Relish

This is a quick-to-make, simple summer relish that uses the glut of radishes everyone gets when they grow them in their garden. It keeps for three to four weeks and is an excellent relish to take on a picnic, just the thing to liven up those sausage rolls, pork pies and cheese sandwiches.

Pick firm young radishes, and make sure you wash them well. I used a processor to chop them, but you could use a board and a sharp knife.

Use a light-coloured vinegar, either white wine vinegar or a distilled malt one. Either should be of 6% acidity.

Yield **approx. 600g** | *Keeps* **3-4 weeks**

425g radishes
1 teaspoon fine sea salt
125g red onion
2 garlic cloves
150ml 6% acidity white wine or distilled malt vinegar
85g white granulated sugar
1 teaspoon mustard seeds
1 teaspoon fennel seeds
1 teaspoon coriander seeds

1. Begin by preparing the radishes. Wash them well and remove any roots, stalks and leaves. **2.** Place the radishes in a food processor and whizz until they are finely chopped. **3.** Put the chopped radishes into a sieve and sprinkle on the salt, mixing it in well. Place the sieve over a bowl and set aside to drain for 30 minutes. **4.** Place some clean jars and their lids on a baking tray and then into the oven preheated to 100°C/200°F/Gas 2 for 20 minutes. **5.** Peel and finely chop the onion and garlic. **6.** Put the vinegar and sugar into a non-reactive, heavy-bottomed pan, and place over a low heat, stirring occasionally until the sugar has dissolved: the mixture should not feel gritty when stirred, and there should be no signs of sugar on the back of your spoon. **7.** Crush the spices, using a pestle and mortar, and add these, the onions and garlic to the vinegar mix. **8.** Squeeze the radishes to get rid of any excess water, then add them to the pan. There is no need to rinse them. **9.** Bring the relish to a simmer, and cook, uncovered, for 10 minutes. **10.** Meanwhile, take the baking tray of jars from the oven, and leave to rest for 5 minutes. **11.** Pot the relish into the hot jars, using a metal spoon and pressing down well. The relish should reach a little up the shoulder of the jar, leaving most of the neck as headspace. The radishes should be pressed below the surface of the vinegar. **12.** Screw the lids on loosely and leave to cool. **13.** Once the relish is cold, check the lids are tight, then label the jars. Store in a cool, dark place, ideally the fridge.

Beetroot Relish

Beetroot have a wonderful colour, and a rich, sweet flavour, so they make a delicious relish. I use ready-cooked beets for this, but if you grow your own, simply boil until you can pierce them with a skewer, then peel and continue with the recipe.

This relish is quick to make, and can be eaten on the day you make it. Everything is chopped fine, using a food processor, but do be careful you don't over-process: you want a textured relish, not a smooth sauce.

I love this relish with cold cuts: rare roast beef or belly pork.

Yield **approx. 800kg** | *Keeps* **4–6 weeks**

450g cooked peeled beetroot

125g onion

100g celery

1 fresh red chilli

1 large orange

200g 6% acidity white wine vinegar

100g raw, light brown sugar

1 teaspoon fine sea salt

1. Place some clean jars and their lids on a baking tray and then into the oven preheated to 100°C/200°F/Gas 2 for 20 minutes. **2.** Cut the beets into quarters, and keep to one side. **3.** Peel and roughly chop the onion. Roughly chop the celery, having removed the strings with a potato peeler. Discard the stem from the chilli, and chop the flesh roughly. **4.** Put the onion, celery and chilli into the bowl of a food processer and whizz until finely chopped. Scrape into a non-reactive, heavy-bottomed saucepan. **5.** Add the quartered beets to the food processor bowl, and whizz these until finely chopped. Add to the vegetables in the pan. **6.** Scrub the orange under hot water using a scourer, and remove the zest using a fine Microplane grater. Add this and the squeezed juice to the pan. **7.** Now stir in the remaining ingredients – the vinegar, sugar and salt – and place the pan over a low heat. Simmer, stirring, until the sugar has dissolved: the mixture should not be gritty when stirred, and there should be no signs of sugar on the back of your spoon. **8.** Bring the relish to a boil, stirring often, then simmer, uncovered, for 10 minutes or until most of the liquid has evaporated. **9.** Meanwhile, remove the baking tray of jars from the oven, and leave to rest for 5 minutes. **10.** Pot the relish into the hot jars, using a metal spoon, and pressing down well. The relish should reach a little up the shoulder of the jar, leaving most of the neck as headspace. **11.** Screw the lids on loosely and leave to cool. **12.** Once the relish is cold, check the lids are tight, then label the jars. Store in a cool, dark place, ideally the fridge.

Preserved Lemons

I've put this recipe here as, whilst these lemons are not exactly a relish, they certainly add relish to any dish you use them in. They are simple to make, but then you must forget about them for three months or so until they are ready, fully cured, and saturated with the salt. This is important for it's the rind and pith you use, scraped clean of the flesh, rinsed of all the salt, then chopped very fine.

I add preserved lemons to sauces, mashed potatoes, mayonnaise, fish dishes (especially fish cakes), curries and North African dishes. Thrifty as ever, I use the salty flesh of the lemons to salt cod, if that's what I'm having for supper, otherwise I simply discard it.

Unwaxed lemons are now readily available in most supermarkets and greengrocers, so I suggest you look for these. If all you can find are waxed lemons, scrub them well using hot water and a brush or scourer.

Store the lemons in glass jars. There is a tendency for the salt to corrode the metal lids or hinges of glass-lidded jars. Just try and wash any salt off the lid each time you use the lemons.

You can slip a red chilli and a couple of bay leaves in down the sides of the jars after you pack the lemons. These don't add to the flavour but, should you be giving the jars as gifts, and they do make lovely gifts, this will look extra pretty.

Use fine sea salt rather than table salt as the latter can contain anti-caking agents such as magnesium carbonate which, though harmless, is unnecessary.

Yield **approx. 1kg** | *Keeps* **2 years**

6–8 medium unwaxed lemons
up to 500g fine sea salt
2 fresh red chillies (optional)
4 fresh bay leaves (optional)

1. Place two clean 500g jars and their lids on a baking tray and then into the oven preheated to 100°C/200°F/Gas 2 for 20 minutes, then allow to cool before using. **2.** Wash the lemons, whether waxed or unwaxed, and then cut them, lengthways, into quarters. **3.** Pack the lemons into the two cold jars lengthways, making sure they are well pressed together. **4.** Add as much salt as you can fit into the jars. **5.** When you are sure you have sufficient salt and lemon slices in the jars, pour a little water into each and screw on the tops. The lemons should be submerged in salty water. **6.** If you want to add chillies or bay leaves, push them down the sides of the jars. **7.** Shake the jars gently. If all the salt dissolves, open the jars and add more. You must always be able to see undissolved salt in the jar. **8.** Take off the lids, rinse off the salt and dry them well, before screwing them back on tightly. **9.** Store the lemons in a cool dark place, checking every few weeks that the salt is still visible and that the lemons are pressed below the surface of the brine. **10.** Leave for three months before using. Store in a cool place. It is not necessary to keep these lemons in the fridge.

Onion & Bacon Relish

You might have heard of this relish as 'bacon jam', which is very popular in voguish restaurants, and is often served with scallops. Bacon jam is similar in composition to a traditional spread that originated in Austria, where a simple mixture of bacon, garlic and salt is processed to form a pâté-like spread. But this is a more complex relish, one that has become immensely popular in Canada and the United States, where maple syrup and fresh coffee are added to the mix, with brown sugar and vinegar helping to extend the short shelf-life.

Make the relish in small batches and store in the fridge. Once you've tasted onion and bacon relish, you'll be amazed at how many dishes you can use it with: it is bliss on toast under melted cheese, it can be used as a garnish on hamburgers; it works with any plainly cooked fish; and would be sensational in a lobster roll. The options are endless.

For maximum impact serve the relish gently warmed in a small pan over a low heat.

Yield **approx. 600g** | *Keeps* **4 weeks**

275g thinly sliced smoked streaky bacon
650g red onions, peeled (you want 500g prepared)
30g garlic
100g raw light muscovado sugar
75ml maple syrup
100ml freshly brewed coffee
100ml 6% acidity white wine vinegar
1 teaspoon chipotle chilli flakes
¼ teaspoon freshly grated nutmeg
¼ teaspoon fresh thyme leaves

1 . Begin by finely slicing the bacon into tiny lardons. Place these in a deep, non-reactive, heavy-bottomed pan. Put this over a moderate heat and cook until the fat is translucent and running into the pan, about 5–7 minutes. **2 .** Meanwhile peel the onions and chop them roughly. Put the chunks in a food processor and whizz until they are finely chopped but not a paste. **3 .** Add the onions to the bacon in the pan, stirring and turning the heat down to low. **4 .** Peel and crush the garlic and add to the pan. Cook, stirring often for about 5 minutes, or until the onions and bacon start to brown. **5 .** Now add all the remaining ingredients and stir well. Simmer, with a lid on, for 1 hour, stirring often. **6 .** Once the relish is thick and soft, remove the lid and simmer until it is thicker still, about another 20 minutes. Stir often to prevent the relish sticking and scorching. **7 .** Meanwhile, place some clean jars and their lids on a baking tray and then into the oven preheated to 100°C/200°F/Gas 2 for 20 minutes. **8 .** Once the relish is thick, pot into the hot jars, using a metal spoon, and pressing down well. The relish should reach a little up the shoulder of the jar, leaving most of the neck as headspace. **9 .** Screw the lids on loosely and leave to cool. **1 0 .** Once the relish is cold, check the lids are tight, then label the jars. Store in the fridge.

SAUCES
& KETCHUPS

Perfect Sauces & Ketchups

Bottled sauces and ketchups are so commonplace that mostly we give them very little thought. Reaching for a bottle of brown sauce to add that all-important finishing touch to a bacon sandwich, or ripping open several sachets of tomato ketchup whenever there are chips to be dipped, we act instinctively, knowing that what we are adding will improve the food immensely.

There are several reasons for this: the spicy sweet-sour tang of the sauce, the juiciness that it adds and, more importantly, the *umami*, that elusive and important fifth taste that I roughly translate as 'age is more interesting than youth'. Add a dollop of sauce or ketchup, and you're adding more than the sum of its ingredients.

What makes a sauce a sauce and not a ketchup? Having spent some considerable time thinking abut this question, I think it's a matter of personal taste: ketchups seems to be a little less serious than sauces, with greengage ketchup being the funky younger sister of rich plum brown sauce. The technique is often similar too: fruit or vegetables are cooked until soft, puréed, sieved, then vinegar, spices and sugar are added and the sauce simmered slowly until thick.

One lovely historical fact about sauces is that they were often quite dreadful when first tasted, but forgotten bottles, with the passage of time, when rediscovered tasted wonderful. Both Tabasco and Worcestershire sauces share this twist of fate, and think how indispensible these two store-cupboard staples are now. I know from personal experience that my brown sauce continues to improve over the years.

I repeat here that the joy of cooking your own food is that you can alter recipes, adding spice or chilli, and cutting back a little on sugar or salt, until the sauce or ketchup is exactly to your taste.

A FEW THINGS TO KNOW ABOUT MAKING SAUCES & KETCHUPS

★ Choose full-flavoured fruit and vegetables, making sure they are not bruised or mouldy. You can make substitutions using like for like. Plums of all shapes and sizes are a good base for both sauces and ketchups. Soft fruit like blueberries and gooseberries are good too.

★ Seasoning with onions, garlic, chilli and ginger is usual, and these are sometimes puréed together before cooking.

★ Cook the fruit and vegetables until very soft. The sauce is puréed and then sieved to give a smooth finish.

★ I have given my preferred vinegars in each recipe. Sauces and ketchups are cooked with sugar and spice as well, so the vinegar can be 5% acidity without it affecting the keeping qualities.

★ Freshly ground spices give another layer of flavour. They can be added before or after the mix is puréed (see individual recipes).

★ It is important to rest the cooked vegetables for a few moments before you blitz them in the liquidiser or food processor, as blending the hot mixture in a machine can be explosive!

★ Once puréed the mixture is rubbed through a sieve. You can choose to use a fine or coarse one; I prefer the latter, as I like my sauces and ketchups to have a thickish body.

★ The purée is put back into a pan, and the sugar is added. Both soft raw brown and white granulated sugars are used here, depending on the flavour I'm trying to achieve. Whatever sugar you choose it must be fully dissolved in your preserve before continuing with the recipe. Timings involved in dissolving sugar will vary, according to sugar type, heat of liquid etc. You must check that the pan no longer feels gritty, and that there are no signs of sugar crystals on your wooden spoon.

★ With a sauce that is simmered until thickened to your liking, remember that it will thicken more as it cools. It is important to stir often during this thickening process to prevent the sauce catching on the bottom of the pan.

★ Allow the sauce to cool a little before potting it up into either glass bottles or jars. These will need to have been washed, dried and sterilised for 20 minutes in an oven preheated to 100ºC/200ºF/Gas 2. Alternatively bottles and rubber seals can be sterilised using a solution such as Milton, following the instructions on the packaging.

★ Bottles for ketchups and sauces are easily bought via mail order. You can find them with either screw-on lids or with hinged stoppers and rubber seals. Glass jars are also perfectly fine, the only constant being that whatever jar or bottle you use, it must have a vinegar-proof lid.

★ When filling the bottles, pour the ketchup or sauce in to a level about 2cm under the lid. Try to keep the neck and rim of the bottles clean, then screw on the tops.

★ Once made, many of the sauces in this chapter are best eaten after they have been stored for about two to three months, during which time the harsh flavours of the vinegar and spices soften to give a wonderfully full-flavoured, dense-textured condiment. While most sauces need time to mature, ketchups can usually be eaten at once.

★ Make sure you label sauces and ketchups carefully, and store them in a cold dark cupboard or pantry.

How to Make the Perfect Bottle of Brown Sauce

Home-made brown sauce is a revelation. I stumbled across the idea of it many years ago when I was searching for a bottle of commercially made brown sauce, and found my favourite one had been discontinued. No demand, I was told, and having insisted that I was indeed demanding it, I went rather grumpily on my way. Later that day I found a recipe that I jiggled about a bit, and have since made every year, serving it with egg and chips, ham and chips and, well, almost anything and chips. My son-in-law also rates it with a full English, or in his case Scottish, breakfast.

You can use any plums in this recipe, which also means that should you run out of the sauce in winter you can always make more, using plums from the southern continents or even frozen ones. I stone the plums before cooking, having found to my sorrow that doing it after cooking is much harder work.

I like to use freshly ground spices as they give the best flavour, and a raw light brown sugar is best. I like fresh chillies and here, as I like the sauce quite fiery, I leave in both the seeds and the pith. If you don't have a liquidiser or processor simply chop the garlic, ginger and chillies finely.

To get your sauce smooth you will need to sieve it. This can be done with a Mouli or the sauce can be liquidised and then rubbed through a coarse sieve. I have a food processor with a purée attachment which is a delight and makes the whole thing simple.

Yield approx. 2.5 litres | *Keeps* 1 year

Ingredients

2kg plums

600g red onions

1 whole garlic bulb

60g fresh root ginger

2–3 fresh hot red chillies, or to taste

200g stoned dates

125g raisins

1 tablespoon coriander seeds

1 teaspoon allspice berries

½ nutmeg

55g sea salt

500ml malt vinegar

To finish

250ml malt vinegar

1 tablespoon ground turmeric

300g raw light muscovado sugar

Equipment

Scales and a measuring jug ★ Chopping board and sharp knife ★ Large heavy-bottomed, non-reactive preserving pan with a lid ★ Food processor with purée attachment ★ Measuring spoons ★ Spice mill or mortar and pestle ★ Wooden spoon ★ Liquidiser and sieve or mouli ★ Glass bottles and/or jars with vinegar-proof lids, washed and dried ★ Baking tray ★ Ladle or funnel ★ Labels

1 . First prepare the fresh ingredients. Cut the plums in half and remove the stones. Put the plums into a large heavy-bottomed, non-reactive preserving pan. **2 .** Peel the onions, chop them into fine dice and put in the pan. **3 .** Now peel all the garlic cloves and the ginger (use the side of a teaspoon), and place these in a food processor with the chillies. Whizz to make a paste. Add this to the plums and onions in the pan. **4 .** Chop the dates and raisins. I find it easiest to do this on a board with a sharp knife. Scrape these into the pan too. **5 .** Now finely grind the spices in a spice mill or mortar and pestle and add these to the pan along with the salt and the 500ml vinegar. **6 .** Put the pan on a low heat and cook until you have reached simmering point, stirring often with a wooden spoon. Once the ingredients start to bubble a little, put on the lid and simmer for 30 minutes or until everything, especially the onion, is very soft. **7 .** Now you need to sieve the sauce to get a smooth purée. Either liquidise the sauce and then rub through a sieve, or you can use a Mouli. Discard all the fibrous matter left in the sieve. If you are lucky enough to have a food processor fitted with a purée attachment, you will find all the detritus is automatically sieved out. **8 .** Place some clean bottles and/or jars and their lids on a baking tray and then into the oven preheated to 100°C/200°F/Gas 2 for 20 minutes. **9 .** Put the purée back into the washed preserving pan and stir in the remaining vinegar, plus the turmeric and sugar. **1 0 .** Place the pan on a low heat, and cook gently, stirring, until the sugar dissolves. **1 1 .** Turn up the heat to medium and simmer, stirring often, until the sauce reduces and thickens. Stir often towards the end of cooking, as the sauce has a tendency to stick to the bottom of the pan and it can burn. **1 2 .** Take the bottles and/or jars from the oven, and leave to rest for 5 minutes. Fill them, using a ladle or funnel, leaving a headspace of about 2cm at the top of each bottle or 1cm at the top of each jar. **1 3 .** Screw the lids on loosely and allow to cool. **1 4 .** When cold label the bottles or jars, and check the lids are tight. Store in a cool, dark place for two to three months before using.

Teriyaki Sauce

I'm having a love affair with this sweet sticky sauce at the moment. I think the increasing presence of Japanese noodle bars on our high streets has made me much more aware of just how versatile this sauce is.

I like to make my own teriyaki sauce, adding fresh ginger, chilli and garlic to the mix. Serve it with pork dishes, stir-fries, noodle dishes, with chicken or with prawns and, best of all, on grilled salmon.

Mirin is a rice wine found in most supermarkets now. You could use a dry sherry in its place.

Yield **approx. 500ml** | *Keeps* **6 months**

30g garlic
60g fresh root ginger
2 fresh red chillies
250ml Japanese soy sauce
250ml mirin (Japanese rice wine)
60g raw soft brown sugar

1 . Place some clean bottles and/or jars and their lids on a baking tray and then into the oven preheated to 100°C/200°F/Gas 2 for 20 minutes. **2 .** Begin by preparing your fresh ingredients. Peel and roughly chop the garlic and ginger. Rough chop the chillies, removing the seeds and pith if necessary. **3 .** In a small blender whizz these three together until you have a smooth paste. **4 .** Scrape this paste into a heavy-bottomed, non-reactive pan, and add the remaining ingredients. **5 .** Place the pan over a low heat and cook gently, stirring, until the sugar has fully dissolved. **6 .** Now turn up the heat and bring the sauce to a simmer. Cook, uncovered, for 20–25 minutes, or until the sauce has thickened slightly. **7 .** Take the bottles and/or jars from the oven, and leave to rest for 5 minutes. Fill them, using a ladle or funnel, leaving a headspace of about 2cm at the top of each bottle or 1cm at the top of each jar. **8 .** Screw the lids on loosely and allow to cool. **9 .** When cold, label the bottles or jars, and check the lids are tight. Store in a cool, dark place. The sauce can be used straightaway.

Smoky Barbecue Sauce

I've been making this barbecue sauce for years, as it tastes exactly as I want it to: sticky, smoky hot and sweet. I use it, diluted with stock or orange juice, to slow-roast spare ribs and belly pork, or straight from the bottle to baste any number of meats, fish and vegetables, whether cooking on the barbecue or under the grill.

Do remember that to avoid cross-contamination you should always pour the sauce into a bowl before using as a baste, never dip the brush in the jar or bottle.

If you can find liquid smoke, do add a teaspoon. It's not essential but, especially if you're not able to use an outdoor grill, it really gives a kick to the finished dish.

Yield **approx. 750ml** | *Keeps* **2 months**

60g fresh root ginger

30g garlic

4 fresh hot red chillies

150ml cider vinegar

250ml apple juice

175g light muscovado sugar

200ml Worcestershire sauce

200ml dark soy sauce

100ml tomato purée

1 teaspoon English mustard powder

1 teaspoon liquid smoke, if available

1 . Place some clean bottles and/or jars and their lids on a baking tray and then into the oven preheated to 100°C/200°F/Gas 2 for 20 minutes. **2 .** Begin by making a purée. Peel the ginger, using the side of a teaspoon, and chop roughly. Peel the garlic and chop the chillies. **3 .** Put all these into a liquidiser and blend until you have a smooth purée. It helps to add a little of the vinegar once the vegetables have been chopped a little. **4 .** Now put all the ingredients into a large heavy-bottomed, non-reactive pan, and whisk them together well. **5 .** Place over a low heat and cook, whisking, until the sugar has dissolved: the mixture should not feel gritty when stirred, and there should be no signs of sugar on the back of your spoon. **6 .** Then turn up the heat until the mixture just simmers. Cook at a simmer for 10–15 minutes until the sauce has reduced and thickened. **7 .** Take the baking tray with the bottles and/or jars from the oven, and leave to rest for 5 minutes. Fill them, using a ladle or funnel, leaving a headspace of about 2cm at the top of each bottle or 1cm at the top of each jar. **8 .** Screw the lids on loosely and allow to cool. **9 .** When cold, label the bottles or jars, and check the lids are tight. Store in a cool, dark place. This sauce can be used at once.

Greengage Ketchup

This ketchup has a fresh, bright flavour. You can serve it with cold dishes, especially pork and chicken, or brush it on to meats on the barbecue, basting them with it about 5 minutes before they are done. I've also brushed it on to both vegetable and white fish kebabs – delicious.

When you are making any smooth ketchup, you will need to sieve it to remove any seeds, stems, bits of spice etc. To make this easier I whizz the mixture first in a liquidiser or processor, which means any hard stones will need to be removed first. I actually find it easier to remove stones from stone fruit *before* cooking.

Choose unblemished fruit for this ketchup if you want a good colour, as bruised greengages go brown very quickly. If you want a milder ketchup, reduce the quantity of chilli; for a hotter one increase it.

Yield **approx. 1.2kg** | *Keeps* **6 months**

1kg greengages
400g onion, prepared weight (about 2 large onions)
150g celery
60g fresh root ginger
40g garlic
40g fresh green chillies
1 tablespoon black peppercorns
1 tablespoon cardamom pods
½ teaspoon celery seeds
1 tablespoon fine sea salt
200ml white wine vinegar
200ml water
250g white granulated sugar

1 . Start by preparing the fruit. Wash the greengages well to remove any dust, then cut them in half and remove and discard the stones. Place them in a large heavy-bottomed, non-reactive pan. **2 .** Chop the onions and the celery finely. The chop does not have to be even, but you want them to be small dice. Add to the pan. **3 .** Peel the ginger, using the side of a teaspoon. Peel the garlic and take the stems from the chillies. Chop all of these roughly. **4 .** Put the ginger, garlic and chilli into a small blender with 2 tablespoons of water and whizz until you have a paste. Scrape this into the pan with the fruit and vegetables. **5 .** Using a spice mill, whizz the peppercorns, cardamom pods and celery seeds until fine. Alternatively crush them as finely as you can in a mortar and pestle. Scrape these into the pan, along with the salt. **6 .** Pour on the vinegar and water, cover the pan and place on a low heat. Cook the fruit and vegetables, stirring often to start with, until they are very soft, about 30 minutes. **7 .** Remove from the heat and allow to sit for 5 minutes, as blending the hot mixture can be explosive! **8 .** Once the ketchup has cooled a little, spoon it into the blender and whizz until smooth. It may be necessary to do this in batches. **9 .** You now need to sieve the ketchup to remove any unwanted lumps, skins, pods etc. Place a sieve over a glass bowl and, using a wooden spoon, rub the mixture through the sieve until you have a dry, fibrous residue left in the sieve. Discard this. **1 0 .** Place some clean jars and/or bottles and their lids on a baking tray and then into the oven preheated to 100°C/200°F/Gas 2 for 20 minutes. **1 1 .** Return the ketchup to the washed saucepan and add the sugar, stirring it in well. **12.** Put the pan over a low heat and stir until the sugar has completely dissolved: the mixture should not feel gritty when stirred, and there should be no signs of sugar on the back of your spoon. **13.** Simmer the ketchup over a medium heat until thick, about 15 minutes, stirring often. The sauce has a tendency to stick to the pan at this stage. **14.** Once it is as thick as you wish, remembering that it will thicken on cooling, remove the pan from the heat and allow it to stand for 5 minutes. Take the baking tray of jars/bottles from the oven at the same time. **15.** Stir the ketchup once more, then pot into the hot jars or bottles, and leaving a headspace of about 2cm at the top of each bottle or 1cm at the top of each jar. **16.** Screw the lids on loosely and allow to cool. **17.** When cold, label the bottles or jars, and check the lids are tight. Store in a cool, dark place. You can use this sauce after a week, but it continues to improve over a month.

Red Pepper Sauce

This pepper sauce has a lovely sweet, hot flavour that I love with steak and chips. The bright red colour brightens up any meal, and the chilli kick is certain to wake up your palate.

There are two ways of preparing the peppers: you can either simply cut them open and take out the pith and seeds then chop them, or if you have more time you can 'roast' them. Hold the peppers over a flame to blacken the skins before peeling, seeding and chopping them.

Yield **approx. 1 litre** | *Keeps* **4 months**

750g ripe red peppers
125g celery
200g red onions
30g garlic
4–6 fresh hot red chillies
1 teaspoon coriander seeds
½ teaspoon celery seeds
250g white wine vinegar
2 teaspoons fine sea salt
200g white granulated sugar

1 . Start by preparing the peppers. Either cut them in half and scrape out the seeds and pith, then chop them roughly before chopping them finely in a food processor. **2 .** Or roast the whole peppers on a fork or skewer over a gas flame or under the grill until blackened on all sides. Place the blackened peppers into a bowl and leave covered with clingfilm for half an hour, as this will help the skins loosen. When the peppers are cool, rub the skins off with your fingers. Cut the peppers open and scrape out the pith and seeds. Chop the peppers finely in a food processor. **3 .** Scrape the peppers into a large heavy-bottomed, non-reactive pan. **4 .** Using a potato peeler, remove the strings from the skin side of the celery and chop the flesh roughly. Put it into the food processor. **5 .** Peel and roughly chop the onion, and peel the garlic. Add these to the celery, along with the roughly chopped chillies. **6 .** Now process the vegetables until finely chopped, then add them to the peppers in the pan. **7 .** Grind the seeds finely in a spice mill, and add these, along with the vinegar, salt and sugar to the pan, and stir well. **8 .** Now put the pan over a low heat and warm the mixture, stirring often until the sugar has dissolved: the mixture should not feel gritty when stirred, and there should be no signs of sugar on the back of your spoon. **9 .** Then turn up the heat and bring the mixture to a simmer. Simmer gently for about 20 minutes until the sauce is thick, stirring often. Remember the sauce will thicken further when cooled. **10 .** Meanwhile, place some clean bottles and/or jars and their lids on a baking tray and then into the oven preheated to 100°C/200°F/Gas 2 for 20 minutes. **11 .** Take the bottles and/or jars from the oven, and leave to rest for 5 minutes. Fill them, using a ladle or funnel, leaving a headspace of about 2cm at the top of each bottle or 1cm at the top of each jar. **12 .** Screw the lids on loosely and allow to cool. **13 .** When cold, label the bottles or jars, and check the lids are tight. Store in a cool, dark place. This sauce can be used at once.

Maple Mustard Sauce

Home-made sauces like this are very simple and require no cooking. They last at least a month if stored in the fridge, and are usually made in small quantities. I like to serve this sauce with grilled gammon steaks, sausages of all kinds, and even spoon it over baked ham as a glaze.

You can grind your own mustard from seeds, using a pestle and mortar. This takes a bit of time, but is really quite satisfying. You could of course bypass the hard work by using a spice mill to grind the mustard seeds, before transferring the powder to a mixing bowl and adding the remaining ingredients. Or you can use a food processor for the entire procedure.

It's best to soak the seeds overnight to soften them, for this I use the vinegar. Be sure to save the vinegar when you drain the seeds, you'll need it later in the recipe.

I love the flavour of tarragon in this mustard sauce, but you could either leave it out or try another herb. Some ground fennel seeds would be nice or even a few chilli flakes if you really like your food hot!

Yield **approx. 350ml** | *Keeps* **up to 6 weeks**

100g mustard seeds
200ml cider vinegar, plus a little extra if needed
75ml maple syrup
1 teaspoon fine sea salt
1 tablespoon dried tarragon leaves

1 . Place the seeds in a glass bowl and pour over the vinegar. Cover the bowl with clingfilm or a tea-towel, and leave overnight. **2 .** Place a large clean glass jar and its lid on a baking tray and then into the oven preheated to 100°C/200°F/Gas 2 for 20 minutes. **3 .** Strain the seeds into the mortar, saving the vinegar for later. Now grind the seeds to a paste with the pestle, adding a little of the reserved vinegar if the paste gets too thick to work. **4 .** Alternatively tip the seeds and 2 tablespoons of vinegar into a food processor and whizz until finely ground. **5 .** Scrape the ground seed paste into a glass bowl and whisk in the vinegar, maple syrup, salt and tarragon. Make sure the sauce is thoroughly mixed. **6 .** Take the jar from the oven, and leave to rest for 5 minutes. Fill it with the sauce, using a large spoon, and leaving a headspace of about 1cm at the top of the jar. **7 .** Screw the lid on loosely and allow to cool. **8 .** When cold, label the jar, and check the lid is tight. Store in the fridge. You could use this sauce at once.

Tomato Ketchup

Home-made tomato ketchup is just delicious, and so very easy to make. There are no artificial flavours or colours, and it is much less sweet than commercial ketchups.

Plus this is a useful recipe to have to hand if you have a glut of ripe tomatoes, or spot a bargain at the greengrocers. You can use any size of tomato and they can be a mix of sizes, the only criteria being that they must be ripe and in good condition. Bruised, squashed or rotten ones have gone too far and won't give a clean fresh flavour. Choose ripe, fleshy red peppers too, as they are full of flavour.

If you are making the ketchup for young children, you may want to consider how much chilli to use. And do grind the spices freshly for the very best flavour.

Yield **approx. 3kg** | *Keeps* **6 months**

3kg ripe tomatoes
400g red peppers
500g onions
200g celery
60g garlic
1–2 fresh red chillies
250ml cider vinegar
225g white granulated sugar

Spice mix
15 cloves
20 allspice berries
1 teaspoon celery seeds
1 x 10cm cinnamon stick, broken into pieces
2 tablespoons coarse sea salt
1 teaspooon black peppercorns

1. Begin by preparing the tomatoes. Wash them under running cold water and them chop them roughly. Place them into your largest, heavy-bottomed, non-reactive pan. **2.** Cut the red peppers in half, and scrape out the seeds and pith. Chop roughly before adding to the tomatoes in the pan. **3.** Peel and chop the onions, and chop the celery, and add them to the pan. **4.** Peel the garlic and roughly chop it and the chillies, adding them to the pan. **5.** Put the spice mix ingredients into a spice mill and whizz until they are finely ground. Put these into the pan along with the vinegar. **6.** Place the pan over a moderate heat, cover with the lid, and simmer gently for about 15–20 minutes or until all the ingredients are very soft. **7.** Remove from the heat and allow to sit for 5 minutes, as blending the hot mixture can be explosive! **8.** Once the ketchup has cooled a little, spoon it into the blender and whizz until smooth. It may be necessary to do this in batches. **9.** You now need to sieve the ketchup to remove any unwanted lumps, skins etc. Place a sieve over a glass bowl and, using a wooden spoon, rub the mixture through the sieve until you have a dry, fibrous residue left in the sieve. Discard this. **10.** Place some clean jars and/or bottles and their lids on a baking tray and then into the oven preheated to 100°C/200°F/Gas 2 for 20 minutes. **11.** Return the ketchup to the washed saucepan and add the sugar, stirring it in well. **12.** Put the pan over a low heat and stir until the sugar has completely dissolved: the mixture should not feel gritty when stirred, and there should be no signs of sugar on the back of your spoon. **13.** Simmer the ketchup over a medium heat until thick, about

15 minutes, stirring often as it has a tendency to stick to the pan at this stage. **14 .** Once it is as thick as you wish, remembering that it will thicken on cooling, remove the ketchup from the heat and allow it to stand for 5 minutes. Take the baking tray of jars/bottles from the oven at the same time. **15 .** Stir the ketchup once more, then pot into the hot jars or bottles, using a ladle or funnel, and leaving a headspace of about 2cm at the top of each bottle or 1cm at the top of each jar. **16 .** Screw the lids on loosely and allow to cool. **17 .** When cold, label the bottles or jars, and check the lids are tight. Store in a cool, dark place. This ketchup is best kept for three to four weeks before being eaten, to allow the flavours to fully mature.

Hoisin Sauce

Exotically spiced, this ubiquitous Chinese plum sauce, when made at home, contains no MSG, and so I find it a much better choice than many commercial brands on sale.

There is no need to add salt here – you will be using soy sauce and that is quite salty enough. When buying soy sauce, choose a Japanese brewed or fermented condiment, rather than a cheaper blended one. Here, as ever, the choice of good-quality ingredients will ensure a great result.

This recipe calls for rice wine vinegar. Look carefully at the label when buying this, as you want the vinegar, not a seasoned condiment. Japanese rice vinegar has an acidity of between 4% and 5%. The condiment is usually around 3%, so is too low for this recipe.

I like a fiery sauce, so use hot red chillies, leaving the seeds and pith in, but you can either use less chilli or take the seeds and pith out before cooking if you prefer something milder.

Use the sauce in stir-fries and other Chinese dishes such as slow-cooked belly pork and spare ribs. I also like to make a faux crispy duck salad using shredded confit duck leg on a salad that contains cucumber and spring onions, adding hoisin sauce to the vinaigrette.

Yield approx. 1.7 litres | *Keeps* 6 months

1 kg ripe plums
300g onions
75g garlic cloves
200g fresh root ginger
1–2 fresh hot red chillies
500ml Japanese rice wine vinegar
6 star anise
500g raw soft brown sugar
100ml dark soy sauce

1 . Begin by preparing the plums. Wash them under cold running water, then cut them in half and remove the stones. Put the prepared plums into a large heavy-bottomed, non-reactive pan. **2 .** Peel and quarter the onions, then peel the garlic. Peel the ginger using the side of a teaspoon, and chop it roughly. Roughly chop the chillies. **3 .** Place the garlic, ginger, chillies and quartered onions into a blender and whizz until you have a finely chopped mixture. **4 .** Scrape this out into the pan with the plums, and add the vinegar. **5 .** Place the pan over a medium heat and bring the mixture up to a simmer. Cover the pan and cook for 20–30 minutes, or until everything is very soft. You will need to stir the pan from time to time. **6 .** Remove from the heat and allow to sit for 5 minutes, as blending the hot mixture can be explosive! **7 .** Meanwhile, put the star anise in a coffee grinder or spice mill, and process until finely ground. Keep to one side. **8 .** Once the sauce has cooled a little, spoon it into the blender and whizz until smooth. It may be necessary to do this in batches. **9 .** You now need to sieve the sauce to remove any unwanted lumps, skins etc. Place a sieve over a glass bowl and, using a wooden spoon, rub the mixture through the sieve until you have a dry, fibrous residue left in the sieve. Discard this. **10.** Place some clean bottles and/or jars and their lids on a baking tray and then into the oven preheated to 100°C/200°F/Gas 2 for 20 minutes. **11.** Return the sauce to the washed saucepan and add the sugar, the finely ground star anise and the soy sauce, stirring well. **12.** Put the pan over a low heat and cook gently, stirring, until the sugar has completely dissolved. **13.** Simmer the sauce over a medium heat until thick, about 15 minutes, stirring often as the sauce has a tendency to stick to the pan at this stage. **14.** Once it is as thick as you wish, remembering that it will thicken on cooling, remove the pan from the heat and allow it to stand for 5 minutes. Remove the bottles and/or jars from the oven at the same time. **15.** Stir the sauce once more, then pot into the hot jars or bottles, using a ladle or funnel, and leaving a headspace of about 2cm at the top of each bottle or 1cm at the top of each jar. **16.** Screw the lids on loosely and allow to cool. **17.** When cold, label the bottles or jars, and check the lids are tight. Store in a cool, dark place. This sauce can be used at once.

Herb Vinegars

Herb vinegars are both simple to make at home, and a wonderful addition to the cook's ingredient palette. I make them using herbs fresh picked from my garden. Vinegar holds the aromatics that herbs have well, thus giving me some summer flavours to use throughout the colder months.

My favourite is tarragon vinegar. Tarragon is a soft aniseed-tasting herb that I love, but the plants soon get leggy and die down, so I pick some and dry the leaves, and use the rest to flavour vinegar. I whisk a little tarragon vinegar into a rich mayonnaise, and dip prawns into it, or add some to *beurre blanc* and use it to anoint a piece of lightly poached turbot.

But you don't have to just choose tarragon, you can use a wide variety of herbs: basil, chervil and rosemary all work well. Pick your chosen herbs, looking for tender fresh shoots, early in the morning, on a dry day when they will be fullest in flavour and when insect activity is at its lowest.

Always use a good-quality mild vinegar – I prefer 6% white wine vinegar, but cider vinegar works well too.

This method uses a double hit of herbs. First you infuse the vinegar with the chopped herb for a week, then you strain it, pour into a clean bottle and tuck in a few fresh herb leaves. Remember to save the bottle to use for the flavoured vinegar.

Yield **approx. 350m** | *Keeps* **1 year**

a good handful of fresh dry, not dried, tarragon leaves
350ml white wine or cider vinegar
2 good sprigs fresh tarragon

1 . Chop the tarragon leaves roughly, and scrape into a glass or china bowl. **2 .** Pour on the vinegar, cover tightly with two layers of clingfilm and leave for seven days in a cool, dark place. **3 .** Now strain the vinegar and discard the herbs. **4 .** Meanwhile, place the washed vinegar bottle and its lid on a baking tray and then into the oven preheated to 100°C/200°F/Gas 2 for 20 minutes. Cool before using. **5 .** Pour the strained vinegar through a funnel into the cold sterilised bottle. Push in the sprigs of fresh tarragon, and close the bottle with a vinegar-proof seal. **6 .** Store the vinegar in a cool, dark place.

Blackberry Ketchup

Blackberry ketchup, deep purple in colour, with a rich fruity flavour, is one the whole family will love. It's not as strange as it might seem: tomatoes and plums are both fruit and they don't get a second glance when it comes to savoury sauces. This ketchup is a perfect match for porky meats: ham, gammon, bacon, sausages, and even Scotch eggs. I also love to eat it with chips, but then I love most things with chips.

Yield **approx. 1kg** | *Keeps* **6 months**

1kg blackberries
350g red onions
30g garlic
1–2 fresh red chillies
1/2 teaspoon celery seeds
1 teaspoon juniper berries
1 teaspoon black peppercorns
500ml cider vinegar
1 teaspoon fine sea salt
400g white granulated sugar

1 . Wash the berries in a colander and shake off as much water as possible. Tip them into a large heavy-bottomed, non-reactive preserving pan. **2 .** Peel and finely chop the onions and the garlic. Chop the chilli. I leave the pith and seeds in, but for a milder flavour take these out. **3 .** Grind the seeds, berries and peppercorns finely, using a spice mill or a mortar and pestle. **4 .** Now put everything but the sugar into the pan with the blackberries. Place this over a moderate heat, and bring the mixture up to a simmer. It should bubble gently. **5 .** Cover with the lid and cook gently for 30–40 minutes or until everything is very soft. Remember to stir from time to time. **6 .** Remove from the heat and allow to sit for 5 minutes, as blending the hot mixture can be explosive. **7 .** Once the ketchup has cooled a little, spoon it into the blender and whizz until smooth. It may be necessary to do this in batches. **8 .** You now need to sieve the ketchup to remove any unwanted lumps, skins etc. Place a sieve over a glass bowl and, using a wooden spoon, rub the mixture through the sieve until you have a dry, fibrous residue left in the sieve. Discard this. **9 .** Place some clean bottles and/or jars and their lids on a baking tray and then into the oven preheated to 100°C/200°F/Gas 2 for 20 minutes. **10 .** Return the ketchup to the washed saucepan and add the sugar, stirring it in well. **11 .** Put the pan over a low heat and stir until the sugar has completely dissolved. **12 .** Simmer the ketchup over a medium heat until thick, about 15 minutes, stirring often, as it has a tendency to stick to the pan at this stage. **13 .** Once it is as thick as you wish, remembering that it will thicken on cooling, remove the ketchup from the heat and allow it to stand for 5 minutes. Take the baking tray of bottles/jars from the oven at the same time. **14 .** Stir the ketchup once more, then pot into the hot jars or bottles, using a funnel, and leaving a headspace of about 2cm at the top of each bottle or 1cm at the top of each jar. **15 .** Screw the lids on loosely and allow to cool. **16 .** When cold, label the bottles or jars, and check the lids are tight. Store in a cool, dark place or the fridge.

Index

ACKNOWLEDGEMENTS

No book is ever the work of one person so in no particular order I want to thank:

Nicky Ross and Sarah Hammond at Hodder for making writing this book a really wonderful experience.

Daisy Goodwin for having the idea of what I think is one of the funniest, most captivating and absolutely the prettiest of television programmes, and then picking me to be a part of it.

Martine Carter for her hard negotiating skills and friendship.

Joy Skipper, who cooks my food almost better than I do and who worked so perfectly with Keiko Oikawa, the most creative of photographers, to create the exquisite pictures in the book.

Bridgette Elwood for making me look beautiful in the pictures.

Georgia Vaux and the entire production team at Hodder who worked so hard to create the look of this book.

Maisie and Gabriel who kept me focused on finishing as promptly as possible so I could book that flight to Seattle.

And finally, my thanks to the wonderful Susan Fleming, my editor and friend, who not only holds my hand, cracks a whip and keeps me in shape, but also makes sure I don't say anything foolish.

First published in Great Britain in 2014 by Hodder & Stoughton An Hachette UK company

1

Copyright © Thane Prince 2014
Photography copyright © Keiko Oikawa 2014

Hardback ISBN 978 1 444 79257 7
Ebook ISBN 978 1 444 79256 0

Editorial Director Nicky Ross
Project Editor Sarah Hammond
Copy Editor Susan Fleming
Design & Art Direction Georgia Vaux
Photographer Keiko Oikawa
Food Stylist Joy Skipper
Props Stylist Jo Harris

Typeset in Roice
Printed and bound in Germany by Mohn Media

Hodder & Stoughton policy is to use papers that are natural, renewable and recyclable products and made from wood grown in sustainable forests. The logging and manufacturing processes are expected to conform to the environmental regulations of the country of origin.

Hodder & Stoughton Ltd
338 Euston Road
London NW1 3BH
www.hodder.co.uk